Mind in a Physical World

Representation and Mind
Hilary Putnam and Ned Block, editors

Representation and Reality by Hilary Putnam

Explaining Behavior: Reasons in a World of Causes by Fred Dretske

The Metaphysics of Meaning by Jerrold J. Katz

A Theory of Content and Other Essays by Jerry A. Fodor

The Realistic Spirit: Wittgenstein, Philosophy, and the Mind by Cora Diamond

The Unity of the Self by Stephen L. White

The Imagery Debate by Michael Tye

A Study of Concepts by Christopher Peacocke

The Rediscovery of the Mind by John R. Searle

Past, Space, and Self by John Campbell

Mental Reality by Galen Strawson

Ten Problems of Consciousness: A Representational Theory of the Phenomenal Mind by Michael Tye

Representations, Targets, and Attitudes by Robert Cummins

Starmaking: Realism, Anti-Realism, and Irrealism edited by Peter J. McCormick

A Logical Journey: From Gödel to Philosophy by Hao Wang

Brainchildren: Essays on Designing Minds by Daniel C. Dennett

Realistic Rationalism by Jerrold J. Katz

The Paradox of Self-Consciousness by José Luis Bermúdez

In Critical Condition: Polemical Essays on Cognitive Science and the Philosophy of Mind by Jerry Fodor

Mind in a Physical World: An Essay on the Mind-Body Problem and Mental Causation by Jaegwon Kim

Mind in a Physical World

An Essay on the Mind-Body Problem and Mental Causation

Jaegwon Kim

A Bradford Book
The MIT Press
Cambridge, Massachusetts

Second printing, 1999

This book was set in Palatino by Wellington Graphics

Printed and bound in the United States of America.

Library of Congress Cataloging-in-Publication Data

Kim, Jaegwon.
  Mind in a physical world : an essay on the mind-body problem and mental causation / Jaegwon Kim.
    p. cm. — (Representation and mind)
  "A Bradford book."
  Book consists of four revised lectures given by the author as the Townsend lectures at the University of California, Berkeley, in Mar. 1996.
  Includes bibliographical references and index.
  ISBN 0-262-11234-5 (hardcover : alk. paper)
  1. Philosophy of mind. 2. Mind and body. 3. Causation.
I. Title. II. Series.
BD418.3.K53 1998
128'.2—dc21   98-24346
                                                                    CIP

Contents

vi   Contents

Preface

This book consists of the four lectures I gave as the Townsend Lectures at University of California, Berkeley, in March, 1996. The texts have been extensively revised since then, but there have been no significant changes in the main points of my claims and arguments. My thanks go to the Berkeley Philosophy Department for the invitation, and for their hospitality during my visit. I benefited from comments and questions from members of the audience, in particular, David Chalmers, Martin Jones, and David Sosa.

In these lectures I tried to set out my current thoughts on a range of issues concerning the metaphysics of the mind—in particular, the mind-body problem, mental causation, and reductionism. The texts were originally written with oral presentation in mind, and I have decided to retain in this final version their somewhat informal and relaxed style of presentation.

These lectures draw materials from the following recent papers of mine: "Mental Causation: What? Me Worry?," *Philosophical Issues* 6 (1995): 123–151; "The Mind-Body Problem: Taking Stock After 40 Years," *Philosophical Perspectives*, 1997; "What is the Problem of Mental Causation?," *Norms and Structures in Science*, ed. M. L. Dalla Chiara et al. (Dordrecht: Kluwer, 1997); "Does the Problem of Mental Causation Generalize?," *Proceedings of the Aristotelian Society*, 1997.

In thinking about the issues discussed here I am indebted to many friends and colleagues who share my interest in philosophy of mind. Who many of them are should be obvious from my texts and notes. I also benefited from spirited comments and challenges from my students at Brown. Maura Geisser, my assistant, has been extremely helpful with her dedicated and efficient work in preparing the manuscript, proofreading, and other tedious but necessary chores. I also want to thank Brown University for its support of my work over the years and my departmental colleagues and students for providing me with a friendly and stimulating environment in which to work.

Providence, Rhode Island
April 1997

Mind in a Physical World

Chapter 1

The Mind-Body Problem: Where We Now Are

Current debates on the mind-body problem can be traced back to the late 1950s and early 1960s. To be more precise, arguably the mind-body problem as we now know it had its origin in two classic papers published one year apart: "The 'Mental' and the 'Physical'" by Herbert Feigl in 1958 and "Sensations and Brain Processes" by J. J. C. Smart the following year.[1] In these papers Smart and Feigl independently proposed an approach to the nature of mind that has come to be called the mind-body identity theory, central-state materialism, the brain state theory, or type physicalism. Although U. T. Place's "Is Consciousness a Brain Process?,"[2] published in 1956, anticipated Smart and Feigl, it was the papers by Smart and Feigl that reintroduced the mind-body problem as a mainstream metaphysical Problematik of analytical philosophy, and launched the debate that has continued to this day. True, Ryle's *The Concept of Mind* was out in 1948, and there were of course Wittgenstein's much debated remarks on mentality and mental language, not to mention a much earlier work by C. D. Broad, *The Mind and Its Place In Nature* (1925).[3] But Ryle's and Wittgenstein's primary concerns were directed at the "logic" of mental discourse rather than the metaphysical problem of explaining how our mentality is related to our physical nature, and moreover Ryle and Wittgenstein, each for different reasons, would have denounced the metaphysical mind-body problem as a piece of philosophical nonsense. In contrast, Broad's work was robustly metaphysical, but unfortunately, it failed to connect with the mind-body debate in the second half of this century, especially in its important early stages.

For many of us who, like me, went to graduate school in the late 1950s and early 1960s, Smart's and Feigl's materialism was our first encounter with the mind-body problem as a systematic philosophical problem. Their approach sounded refreshingly bold and tough-minded, and seemed in tune with the optimistic scientific temper of the times. It was an intriguing and exciting idea that mental events could just *be* brain processes, and that scientific research could show this, just as science showed us that light was electromagnetic radiation, and that genes were DNA molecules. But the identity theory was unexpectedly short-lived—its precipitous fall began only several years after its introduction. It is clear in retrospect, though, that despite its short life, the theory made one crucial contribution that has outlasted its reign as a theory of the mind. What I have in mind is the fact that the brain state theory helped set the basic parameters and constraints for the debates that were to come—a set of broadly physicalist assumptions and aspirations that still guide and constrain our thinking today. One indication of this is the fact that when the brain state theory began fading away in the late 1960s and early 1970s few lapsed back into Cartesianism or other serious forms of mind-body dualism. Almost all the participants in the debate have stayed with physicalism, and even those who had a major hand in the demise of the Smart-Feigl materialism have continued their allegiance to a physicalist worldview. Through the 1970s and 1980s and down to this day, the mind-body problem—*our* mind-body problem—has been that of finding a place for the mind in a world that is fundamentally physical. The shared project of the majority of those who have worked on the mind-body problem over the past few decades has been to find a way of accommodating the mental within a principled physicalist scheme, while at the same time preserving it as something distinctive—that is, without losing what we value, or find special, in our nature as creatures with minds.

What made the demise of the mind-brain identity theory so quick and seemingly painless, causing few regrets and second thoughts among philosophers, was the fact the two principal objections that overthrew it, the multiple realization argument advanced by Hilary Putnam[4] and the anomalist argument of Donald Davidson,[5] contained within them seeds for appealing alternative pictures of mentality, namely functionalism and anomalous monism. The core idea of functionalism, that mental kinds and properties are functional kinds at a higher level of abstraction than physicochemical or biological kinds, was a suggestive and eye-opening idea that seemed to help us make sense of cognitive science, which was being launched about the same time. The functionalist approach to mentality seemed made to order for the new science of mentality and cognition, for its central doctrine seemed to postulate a distinctive domain of mental/cognitive properties that could be scientifically investigated independently of their physical/biological implementations—an idea that promised for psychology both legitimacy and autonomy as a science. Functionalism provided the new science of cognition with both a metaphysics and a methodology.

Davidson's anomalous monism, too, offered us another appealing package, although its special attractions were different from those of functionalism. On the one hand, it told us that the mental domain, on account of its essential anomalousness and normativity, cannot be the object of serious scientific investigation,[6] placing the mental on a wholly different plane from the physical. In particular, its anomalousness vis-à-vis the physical—that is, the impossibility of laws connecting mental kinds with physical kinds—was thought to entail the irreducibility of mental kinds to physical kinds. This meant that mental kinds are distinct from physical or biological kinds, contradicting the Smart-Feigl mind-body identity thesis. In this way Davidson's anomalous monism secured for us the autonomy of the mental, although for reasons that are different from those offered by functionalism. On the other hand, the monistic component of anomalous monism insisted that all individual events ("token events") are physical events subject to laws of physics, thereby giving the physical the pride of place in our ontology. This assuaged our physicalist aspirations. Each in its own distinctive way, therefore, both anomalous monism and functionalism made it possible for us to shed the restrictive constraints of monolithic reductionism without losing our credentials as physicalists. Or so it seemed.

Supervenience, Realization, and Emergence

What do these two doctrines, anomalous monism and functionalism, say about the mind-body problem, the problem of how the mental and the physical are related? Anomalous monism is a physicalist monism that holds that every individual mental event is a physical event, but it also maintains that the mental is anomalous, that is, not governed by laws (or "strict laws," as Davidson sometimes puts it). In particular, it famously claims that there are no laws connecting mental kinds or properties with physical ones. This component of the doctrine, the anomalousness of the mental in relation to the physical, is a *negative* thesis: it tells us how the mental is *not* related to the physical, and says nothing about how the two *are* related. The burden therefore falls on the first component of the doctrine—the claim that every mental event is a physical event—to tell us a positive story about the relationship between the mental and the physical.

But exactly what does Davidson's physical monism tell us about the mind-body relation? The answer is: much less than what one might have expected. For Davidson, the content of the claim that all mental events are physical events turns out to be only this: every event that can be given a mental description can also be given a physical description, or, as we might say in current idiom, that every event that has a mental property (or falls under a mental kind) also has a physical property (falls under a physical kind). For, within Davidson's scheme, an event is physical or mental only as it is describable in the physical or mental vocabulary, or as it falls under a physical or a mental kind. So Davidson's monism comes to this proposition: there are no events that have only mental properties (descriptions), although there may be, and presumably are, events with physical properties (descriptions) only. This requires no type-type connections between mental and physical kinds, and Davidson's doctrine of mental anomalism specifically prohibits nomological (or any stronger) linkages between mental types and physical types. But a doctrine that outlaws type-type, or property-property, connections between the mental and the physical is one that in effect says there is no connection between our mental nature and our physical nature. This means that the monism of anomalous monism is no less a negative thesis than the anomalism of anomalous monism.

That anomalous monism doesn't say much about the mind-body relation can be seen from an analogy. Consider the statement, which presumably is true, that every object that has a color has a shape—or to put it in a way that is parallel to Davidson's monism, every object with a color is identical with an object with a shape. Clearly this statement says nothing about the relation between colors and shapes; in fact we know there are no interesting connections between them. Analogously in the mind-body case, the statement that every event with a mental property is an event with a physical property says nothing about—and it is designed by Davidson to say nothing about—the presence or absence of type-type connections between the mental and the physical. This means that Davidson's anomalous monism says no more about the relationship between the mental and the physical than the claim that all objects with a color have a shape says about the relationship between colors and shapes. As far as anomalous monism goes then, there need be no systematic relationships between mental properties and physical properties—any more than between the colors and shapes of things around us. The same holds for any version of the so-called token physicalism similar to Davidson's physical monism.[7] I believe we want our mind-body theories to tell us more, a *positive* story about how mental properties and physical properties *are* related, and hopefully also explain why they are so related. We don't get such a story from anomalous monism.

This may well have been what led Davidson, in his "Mental Events," to invoke mind-body supervenience. After developing his argument for the impossibility of laws connecting the mental and the physical, he adds in a somewhat offhanded way:

> Although the position I describe denies there are psycho-
> physical laws, it is consistent with the view that mental
> characteristics are in some sense dependent, or superven-
> ient, on physical characteristics. Such supervenience might
> be taken to mean that there cannot be two events alike in
> all physical respects but differing in some mental respects,
> or that an object cannot alter in some mental respect with-
> out altering in some physical respect.[8]

Although the British emergentists early in this century appear
to have been the first to use the expression "supervenience" in
connection with the mind-body problem and the concept had
been around for some time in ethical theory, the passage just
cited signaled the introduction of the supervenience idiom into
the contemporary debate on the mind-body problem. In any
case mind-body supervenience understood in some such sense
as Davidson's quickly caught on, I believe, precisely because it
gave, or at least promised to give, a statement of how the mental
and the physical *are* related to each other. Note, in particular,
the fact that supervenience concerns mental and physical *properties* and *kinds* (or "characteristics" or "respects," in Davidson's
words), not mental and physical tokens or Davidsonian events
as structureless particulars. Unlike the two central theses of
anomalous monism, the supervenience claim therefore finally
says something positive about the relationship between mental
and physical properties.

Moreover the supervenience claim is physicalistically appealing: an asymmetric dependence of the mental on the physical is
clearly implied, if not stated outright. This mind-body dependence relation was thought (in fact, explicitly claimed by Davidson and others) to be consistent with the irreducibility of the
mental to the physical. It is fair to say, I think, that the supervenience idea, which Davidson seemed to toss off almost like an
afterthought and which he did little to explain or elaborate,
much less defend, came to overshadow the core doctrines of
anomalous monism, creating a new focus and direction for the
physicalist program. Whether mind-body supervenience is to be

thought of as an integral component of Davidson's anomalous monism is not a question that concerns us here.[9] Whatever we may want to say about that question, the fact remains that philosophers found a promising physicalist metaphysics in mind-body supervenience rather than in the two theses of anomalous monism, that is, physicalist event monism and the anomalism of the mental. That is why the supervenience idea took off, in the late 1970s, with a life of its own in the mind-body debate.

Functionalists, by and large, were not metaphysicians, and few of them were self-consciously concerned about just what their position entailed about the mind-body problem.[10] The key term the mainstream functionalists used to describe the relation between mental properties (kinds, states, etc.) and physical properties was "realization" (or sometimes "implementation," "execution," etc.): mental properties are "realized" or "implemented" by (or in) physical properties, though neither identical nor reducible to them. But the term "realization" was introduced,[11] and quickly gained currency, chiefly on the strength of computational analogies (in particular, the idea that abstract, mathematically characterized computing machines are realized in concrete physical/electronic devices), and few functionalists, especially in the early days, made an explicit effort to explain what the realization relation consisted in—in particular, what this relation implied as regards the traditional options on the mind-body problem.

I believe that the idea of supervenience was embraced by some functionalists, and those influenced by the multiple realization argument, in part because it promised to fill this metaphysical void. The thesis that mental properties are supervenient on physical properties seemed to fit the metaphysical requirements of functionalism very nicely: it promised to give a clear sense to the primacy of the physical domain and its laws, thereby doing right by the physicalist commitments of most functionalists—and this without implying physical reductionism, thereby protecting the autonomy of the mental. Further, in allowing multiple supervenience bases for supervenient properties, it

offered a perfect scheme for accommodating the multiple realizability of mental properties.

I believe this is why many philosophers, including those who
espoused the functionalist outlook, saw in mind-body supervenience a satisfying metaphysical statement of physicalism without
reductionism. This helped to create, in the mid- to late 1970s,
what Ned Block has called "the antireductionist consensus"[12]
and its subsequent entrenchment. This position, now standardly
called "nonreductive physicalism" (or "nonreductive materialism"), has been, and still is, the most influential metaphysical
position, not only on the mind-body problem but more generally
on the relationship between higher-level properties and underlying lower-level properties in all areas. Thus the approach
yielded as a bonus a general philosophical account of how the
special sciences are related to basic physics: properties in the
domain of the special sciences—properties in terms of which
laws and explanations in these sciences are formulated—are supervenient on basic physical properties but not reducible to
them, and in this sense the special sciences are autonomous from
basic physics. If you are a scientist outside basic physics, it is
probably comforting to know that you can do your science independently of what goes on in theoretical physics, and that you
can formulate laws and explanations in your special discipline
in its own distinctive vocabulary that need not answer to that of
physics. Of course this is what scientists outside basic physics
generally do anyway, but it's nice to have a philosophical rationale for it.

In any case, one direct consequence of the entrenchment of the
antireductionist consensus has been the return of emergentism—
if not all the florid doctrines of classic emergentism of the 1920s
and 1930s, at least its distinctive vocabulary and slogans. In the
heyday of positivism and "unity of science," emergentism used
to be relegated to the heap of unsavory pseudoscientific doctrines, not quite as disreputable as, say, neo-vitalism with its
entelechies and élan vital, but nearly as obscure and incoherent.
With the demise of reductive physicalism, emergentism has been
showing strong signs of a comeback.[13] We now see an increasing

and unapologetic use of expressions like "emergent," "emergent property," and "emergent phenomenon," seemingly in the sense intended by the classic emergentists, not only in serious philosophical literature[14] but in the writings in psychology, cognitive science, systems theory, and the like.[15]

To sum up, then, three ideas have been, and still are, prominent in discussions of the mind-body problem since the demise of the reductive brain-state theory: the idea that the mental "supervenes" on the physical, the idea that the mental is "realized" by the physical, and the idea that the mental is "emergent" from the physical. Exploration of these three ideas, and the roles they play in debates on the mind-body problem, will be one of the things I want to do in these lectures. Today I will focus on supervenience and realization. I will say something about emergence along the way as my talks proceed, and especially in connection with my discussion of reduction and reductionism in a later talk (chapter 4).[16]

Supervenience Is Not a Mind-Body Theory

Let us begin with supervenience. Supervenience is standardly taken as a relation between two sets of properties, the supervenient properties and their base properties. As is by now well known, a variety of supervenience relations is available; for our purposes we may focus on what is called "strong supervenience." Consider then the following thesis of mind-body supervenience:

> Mental properties *supervene* on physical properties, in that necessarily, for any mental property M, if anything has M at time t, there exists a physical base (or subvenient) property P such that it has P at t, and necessarily anything that has P at a time has M at that time.

For example, if a person experiences pain, it must be the case that that person instantiates some physical property (presumably, a complex neural property) such that whenever anyone instantiates this physical property, she must experience pain.

That is, every mental property has a physical base that guarantees its instantiation. Moreover, without such a physical base, a mental property cannot be instantiated. Under certain assumptions concerning property composition, a supervenience thesis stated this way (sometimes called "the modal operator" formulation) can be shown to be equivalent to another familiar formulation of supervenience (sometimes called "the possible world" or "indiscernibility" definition):

> Mental properties *supervene* on physical properties, in that necessarily any two things (in the same or different possible worlds) indiscernible in all physical properties are indiscernible in mental respects.

Or we can say: any two things that are exact physical duplicates necessarily are exact psychological duplicates as well—that is, physical duplicates are duplicates *tout court*. Or, as some have put it: no mental difference without a physical difference.[17] We will consider these two formulations of mind-body supervenience to be equivalent[18] and use one or the other to suit the context.

Under mind-body supervenience a physical base property, P, for mental property M guarantees, as a matter of necessity, the occurrence of M; that is, necessarily if something instantiates P, it instantiates M. The modal force of necessity involved is a parameter to be fixed to suit one's view of the mind-body relation; some may go for metaphysical or even logical/conceptual necessity, while others will settle for nomological necessity. (We should keep in mind that the modal force of supervenience may vary for different groups of mental properties; for example, it is possible for intentional properties to supervene with logical/conceptual necessity, while phenomenal properties supervene only with nomological necessity.) As has been noted, one and the same mental property may have multiple physical bases: an instance of pain in a human may be grounded in one neural property, and another instance of pain, say in a reptile, may be grounded in another.

As we saw in Davidson, it is customary to associate supervenience with the idea of *dependence* or *determination*: if the mental supervenes on the physical, the mental is dependent on the physical, or the physical determines the mental, roughly in the sense that the mental nature of a thing is entirely fixed by its physical nature. Sometimes this is put in terms of "worlds": the psychological character of a world is determined entirely by its physical character—as it is often put, worlds that are physically indiscernible are psychologically indiscernible. The relation of dependence, or determination, is asymmetric: if x depends on, or is determined by y, it cannot be that y in turn depends on or is determined by x. What does the determining must be taken to be, in some sense, ontologically prior to, or more basic than, what gets determined by it. But mind-body supervenience as stated isn't asymmetric; in general, the supervenience of A on B does not exclude the supervenience of B on A. The notion of supervenience we introduced simply states a pattern of *covariance* between the two families of properties, and such covariances can occur in the absence of a metaphysical dependence or determination relation. For example, two sets of properties may show the required covariance because each depends on a third, somewhat in the manner in which two collateral effects of the single cause exhibit a pattern of lawful correlation. What needs to be added to property covariance to get dependence or determination, or whether dependence/determination must be taken as an independent primitive, are difficult questions that probably have no clear answers. We will simply follow the customary usage and understand supervenience to incorporate a dependence/determination component as well. In fact common expressions like "supervenience base" and "base property" all but explicitly suggest asymmetric dependence.

Suppose then that the mental supervenes on the physical. Does this give us a possible account of how our mentality is related to the physical nature of our being? That is, can we use supervenience itself to state a philosophical theory of the way minds are related to bodies? It has sometimes been thought—as

I myself did at one point—that the answer is yes, that what might be called supervenience physicalism is a possible position to take on the mind-body problem. There has been a controversy concerning whether supervenience, in the sense of strong supervenience, is indeed consistent with the irreducibility of the supervenient properties to their subvenient bases. But the discussion of this question has been inconclusive,[19] and I now believe that the debate was framed in terms of a seriously flawed notion of reduction (see chapter 4). Here we will focus on the question whether or not mind-body supervenience as such can be thought of as an account of the mind-body relation.

Brief reflection shows that the answer is no, that mind-body supervenience in itself does not give us a theory of the mind-body relation. There are at least two related reasons for this. First, mind-body supervenience is consistent with a host of classic positions on the mind-body problem; in fact it is a shared commitment of many mutually exclusionary mind-body theories. As we will see, both emergentism and the view that the mental must be physically realized—that is, there can be no nonphysical realizations of mental properties (we can call this physical realizationism)—imply mind-body supervenience. But emergentism is a form of dualism that takes mental properties to be nonphysical intrinsic causal powers, whereas physical realizationism, as I will argue, is a monistic physicalism. What is more obvious, type physicalism, which reductively identifies mental properties with physical properties, implies mind-body supervenience. Moreover epiphenomenalism, viewed by some physicalists, for example, J. J. C. Smart, as their chief dualistic rival, is apparently committed to mind-body supervenience: if two organisms differ in some mental respect, that must be because they differ in some physical respect—it must be because the physical cause of the mental respect involved is present in one but absent from the other. That is, the epiphenomenalist would surely agree that two physically indistinguishable organisms must manifest the same mental characteristics. If mind-body supervenience is a commitment of each of these diverse, and conflicting, approaches to the mind-body problem, it cannot itself be a position on this problem that can be set alongside these classic alternatives.[20]

What this shows is that the mere claim of mind-body supervenience leaves unaddressed the question what *grounds* or *accounts for* it—that is, the question why the supervenience relation should hold for the mental and the physical.[21] To see the general issue involved here, consider normative supervenience, the widely accepted doctrine that normative or evaluative properties supervene on nonnormative, nonevaluative properties. Various metaethical positions accept normative supervenience but offer differing accounts of its provenance. For the ethical naturalist, the supervenience holds because normative properties are definable in terms of nonnormative, naturalistic properties. An ethical intuitionist like G. E. Moore would see normative supervenience as a fundamental synthetic a priori fact not susceptible to further explanation; it is something we directly apprehend through our moral sense. R. M. Hare, a noncognitivist, would attempt to tie it with certain regulative constraints on the language of prescription. Still others may try to ground it in the very idea of normative evaluation: normative judgments and evaluations must ultimately be based on reasons or grounds that are themselves nonnormative and nonevaluative, and this means that normative properties must have nonnormative criteria of application. In the mind-body case, too, we can think of rival mind-body theories as offering competing explanations of mind-body supervenience. The explanation offered by reductive type physicalism is analogous to the naturalistic explanation of normative supervenience—mind-body supervenience holds because mentality is physically reducible. On type physicalism, mental properties *are* physical properties, just as on ethical naturalism ethical properties *are* natural properties. Emergentism, like ethical intuitionism, views mind-body supervenience as something that admits no explanation; it is a brute fact that must be accepted with "natural piety," as a leading emergentist, Samuel Alexander, urged. In contrast, epiphenomenalism would invoke the causal relation (the "same cause, same effect" principle) to explain supervenience, while on physical realizationism mind-body supervenience is a direct consequence of the fact that mental properties are, as we will see, second-order functional properties defined over first-order physical properties, and so on.

We must conclude then that mind-body supervenience itself is not an *explanatory theory*; it merely states a pattern of property covariation between the mental and the physical and points to the existence of a dependency relation between the two. Yet supervenience is silent on the nature of the dependence relation that might explain why the mental supervenes on the physical. Another way of putting the point would be this: supervenience is not a *type* of dependence relation—it is not a relation that can be placed alongside causal dependence, reductive dependence, mereological dependence, dependence grounded in definability or entailment, and the like. Rather, any of these dependence relations can generate the required covariation of properties and thereby qualify as a supervenience relation. Supervenience therefore is not a metaphysically "deep" relation; it is only a "phenomenological" relation about patterns of property covariation, patterns that possibly are manifestations of some deeper dependence relationships. If this is right, mind-body supervenience *states* the mind-body problem—it is not a solution to it. This means that nonreductive physicalism must look elsewhere for its metaphysical grounding; supervenience itself is not capable of supplying it. Any putative account of the mind-body relation that accepts mind-body supervenience must specify a dependence relation between the mental and physical that is capable of grounding and explaining mind-body supervenience.

These considerations, however, need not be taken to be seriously deflationary about the usefulness of the supervenience idea in the philosophy of mind. They certainly deflate the hope that supervenience itself might give us an account of the mind-body relation. But there is also a positive side: our considerations indicate that mind-body supervenience captures a commitment common to all positions on the nature of mentality that are basically physicalistic. For it represents the idea that mentality is at bottom physically based, and that there is no free-floating mentality unanchored in the physical nature of objects and events in which it is manifested. This is an idea that can be shared by many diverse positions on the mind-body problem, from reductive type physicalism at one extreme to dualistic emergentism at the other. In contrast, mind-body supervenience is inconsistent with more extreme forms of dualism, such as, Cartesian dualism, which allow the mental world to float freely, unconstrained by the physical domain.[22] Thus mind-body supervenience can serve as a useful dividing line: it can be viewed as defining *minimal physicalism*.

The Layered Model and Mereological Supervenience

Cartesian substance dualism pictures the world as consisting of two independent domains, the mental and the material, each with its own distinctive defining properties (consciousness and spatial extendedness, respectively). There are causal interactions across the domains, but entities in each domain, being "substances," are ontologically independent of those of the other, and it is metaphysically possible for one domain to exist in the total absence of the other. What has replaced this picture of a dichotomized world is the familiar multilayered model that views the world as stratified into different "levels," "orders," or "tiers" organized in a hierarchical structure. The bottom level is usually thought to consist of elementary particles, or whatever our best physics is going tell us are the basic bits of matter out of which all material things are composed.[23] As we go up the ladder, we successively encounter atoms, molecules, cells, larger living organisms, and so on. The ordering relation that generates the hierarchical structure is the mereological (part-whole) relation: entities belonging to a given level, except those at the very bottom, have an exhaustive decomposition, without remainder, into entities belonging to the lower levels. Entities at the bottom level have no physically significant proper parts.

It is part of this layered picture that at each level there are properties, activities, and functions that make their first appearance, or "emerge," at that level (we may call them the characteristic properties of that level). Thus among the characteristic properties of the molecular level are electrical conductivity, inflammability, density, viscosity, and the like; activities and functions like metabolism and reproduction are among the characteristic properties of the cellular and higher biological levels; and consciousness and other mental properties make their appearance at the level of higher organisms. For much of this century, a layered picture of the world like this has formed a constant—tacitly assumed if not explicitly stated—backdrop for debates on a variety of issues in metaphysics and philosophy of science—for example, reduction and reductionism, the mind-body problem, emergence, the status of the special sciences, and the possibility of a unified science. In fact this picture has had a strong and pervasive influence on the way we formulate problems and their possible solutions in many areas. Sometimes the layered model is couched in terms of concepts and languages rather than entities and their properties. Talk of levels of *organization*, *descriptions* or *languages*, of *analysis*, of *explanation*, and the like is encountered everywhere—it has thoroughly permeated primary scientific literature in many fields, in particular, various areas of psychology and cognitive science, systems theory, and computer science—as well as philosophical writings about science.[24]

Now we come to a crucial question: How are the characteristic properties of a given level related to the properties at the adjacent levels—in particular, to those at the lower levels? How are biological ("vital") properties related to physicochemical properties? How are consciousness and intentionality related to biological/physical properties? How are social phenomena, phenomena characteristic of social groups, related to phenomena involving individual members? As you will agree, these are among the central questions of philosophy of science, metaphysics, and philosophy of mind. Possible answers to them define the philosophical options on the issues involved. Some of the well-known major alternatives include reductionism, antireductionism, methodological individualism, emergentism, neo-vitalism, and the like. You may attempt to give a single uniform answer applicable to all pairs of adjacent levels, or you may take different positions regarding different levels. For example, you might argue that properties at every level (higher than the bottom level) are reducible, in some clear and substantial sense, to lower-level properties and therefore ultimately to the basic properties of physics, or you might restrict the reductionist claim to certain selected levels (say, biological properties in relation to physicochemical properties) and defend an antireductionist stance concerning properties at other levels (say, consciousness and intentionality). And it isn't even necessary to give a uniform answer in regard to all characteristic properties of a given level; concerning mental properties, for example, it is possible to hold that phenomenal properties, or qualia, are irreducible, while holding intentional properties, including propositional attitudes, to be reducible (say, causal/functionally or biologically).

Let us now look at the layered model with supervenience in mind. When supervenience is superposed on the layered model, something like the following emerges as a general schema of supervenience claims about properties at a given level (other than the lowest one) in relation to those at lower levels:

> For any x and y, belonging to level L (other than the lowest level), if x and y are indiscernible in relation to properties at all levels lower than L (or, as we may say, x and y are *microindiscernible*), then x and y are indiscernible with respect to all properties at level L.

How do we explain the idea of *microindiscernibility*? The following seems pretty natural and straightforward:[25]

> x and y, belonging to level L, are *microindiscernible* if and only if for every decomposition D of x into proper parts belonging to lower levels, y has an isomorphic decomposition C in the sense that there is a one-one function I from D to C such that for any n-adic property or relation P at levels lower than L, $P(\mathbf{d}_n)$ iff $P(I(\mathbf{d}_n))$, where $\mathbf{d}_n$ is any n-tuple of elements in D and $I(\mathbf{d}_n)$ is the image of $\mathbf{d}_n$ under I, and conversely from y to x.

Not surprisingly, supervenience theses, when applied to the layered model, turn into claims of *mereological supervenience*, the doctrine that properties of wholes are fixed by the properties and relations that characterize their parts. A general claim of macro-micro supervenience then becomes the Democritean atomistic doctrine that the world is the way it is because the microworld is the way it is.[26]

Let us now return to mental properties. Presumably mental properties arise as characteristic properties at the level of higher organisms, and like any other high-level properties, they are supervenient in the sense explained, on the lower-level properties characterizing their proper parts. That is, if M is a mental property had by something x, then any y that is microindiscernible from x will also have M. Mental properties, therefore, are macroproperties supervening on microproperties.

We should resist the temptation to read more into this result than what's really there. On the layered model, mind-body supervenience is an instance of *mereological supervenience*, and this might seem like an advance, tempting us into thinking that we might try explaining mind-body supervenience in parallel with the way macrophysical properties are determined and explained by microphysical properties. But supervenience or determination is one thing, explanation quite another. We may know that B determines A (or A supervenes on B) without having any idea why this is so—why A should arise from B, not C, or why A, rather than D, arises from B. Mereological supervenience of the mental on the physical would not automatically promise us an intelligible account of why the particular mind-body supervenience relations hold. Given that mental property M is supervenient on a certain physical mereological configuration P, the questions still remain: Is M reducible to P in some appropriate sense? Can we explain why something has M in terms of its having P? Are the P-M and other such supervenience relations further explainable (and what can "explanation" mean here?), or must they be taken as brute and fundamental? These questions are independent of the question whether P is a microphysically characterized property.

These, I believe, are legitimate questions. The layered model provides us with a useful ontological scheme within which we can situate the mind-body problem. By placing the problem in the broader context of this model, we give it both generality and structure, and this raises the hope that we will be able to set some nonarbitrary parameters and constraints on the resolution of the problem, and to appreciate its possible distinctiveness as well as its commonality with problems in other areas. But the hard questions remain untouched. Let us now turn to the idea of physical realization as an approach to these questions.

Physical Realizationism

As you may recall, by physical realizationism I mean the claim that mental properties, if they are realized, must be physically realized—that is, no mental properties can have nonphysical realizations.[27] The thesis therefore is equivalent to the conjunction of physicalism with the functionalist conception of mental properties, and "physicalist functionalism" would be an equally good name for this position. Functionalism takes mental properties and kinds as functional properties, properties specified in terms of their roles as causal intermediaries between sensory inputs and behavioral outputs, and the physicalist form of functionalism takes physical properties as the only potential occupants, or "realizers," of these causal roles.[28] To use a stock example, for an organism to be in pain is for it to be in some internal state that is typically caused by tissue damage and that typically causes groans, winces, and other characteristic pain behavior. In this sense being in pain is said to be a second-order property: for a system x to have this property is for x to have some first-order property P that satisfies a certain condition D, where in the present case D specifies that P has pain's typical causes and typical effects.

More generally, we can explain the idea of a second-order property in the following way.[29] Let $\mathbf{B}$ be a set of properties; these are our first-order (or "base") properties. They are not first-order in any absolute sense; they may well be second-order relative to another set of properties.[30] When mental properties are to be generated out of **B** as second-order properties, we must of course take **B** to consist of nonmental properties (including physico-chemical, biological, and behavioral properties[31]). We then have this:

> F is a *second-order property* over set **B** of base (or first-order) properties iff F is the property of having some property P in **B** such that $D(P)$, where D specifies a condition on members of **B**.

Second-order properties therefore are second-order in that they are generated by *quantification*—existential quantification in the present case—over the base properties. We may call the base properties satisfying condition D the realizers of second-order property F. For example, if the base set **B** comprises colors, then *the property of having a primary color* can be thought of as a second-order property: having a property P in **B** such that $P =$ red or $P =$ blue or $P =$ green.[32] Thus being red, being blue, and being green are the three realizers of having a primary color. If **B** is a set of minerals,[33] being jade can be thought of as the second-order property of being a mineral that is pale green or white in color and fit for use as gemstones or for carving. This second-order property has two known realizers, jadeite and nephrite.

We need to say something about the vocabulary allowed for formulating condition D; for present purposes we will assume that the causal/nomological relation (holding for properties—or property instances, to be exact) is available, in addition to the usual logical expressions and appropriate descriptive terms (e.g., those referring to members of **B**). We may now explain *functional properties* over **B** as those second-order properties over **B** whose specification D involves the causal/nomic relation. That is, functional properties are second-order properties defined in terms of causal/nomic relations among first-order properties. An example of a functional property is dormitivity[34]: a substance has this property just in case it has a chemical property that causes people to sleep. Both Valium and Seconal have dormitivity but in virtue of different first-order (chemical) realizers—diazepam and secobarbital, respectively. Or consider *water-solubility*: something has this property just in case it has some property P such that when it is immersed in water P causes it to dissolve. This conception of functional property accords well with the standard usage in the functionalist literature. On the functionalist conception, mental properties are specified by causal roles, that is, in terms of causal relations holding for first-order physical properties (including biological and behavioral properties). In this sense mental properties turn out to be *extrinsic* or *relational* properties of individuals that have them. To be in a mental state is to be in a state with such-and-such as its typical causes and such-and-such as its typical effects. Whether or not a given property qualifies as an occupant of a specified role—that is, whether or not it is a realizer of a functional property—depends essentially on its causal/nomological relations to other properties, not on its intrinsic character. Intrinsic characters do matter of course, but only because of their capacity to get causally hooked up with other properties. Thus we may think of intrinsic characters as representing the causal potentials of their bearers (relative to the prevailing laws) which help determine whether or not their bearers instantiate a given functional property. On the other hand, networks of causal/nomological relations are constitutive of functional properties.[35]

If mental properties are functional properties, they are therefore not tied, definitionally or constitutively, to the compositional/structural details of their realizers. Whether a given property realizes a given functional property is a contingent, empirical question; any base properties with the right causal/nomological relations to other properties can serve as its realizers. And any mechanism that gets activated by the right input and that, when activated, triggers the right response serves as a realizer of a psychological capacity or function. It has long been a platitude in philosophy of mind/psychology, and philosophical discussions of the special sciences, that mental properties and other special science properties can have extremely diverse realizers in different species and structures. This observation has promoted a certain view about the nature of psychology and cognitive science, namely that the formal/abstract character of mental properties, standardly taken to be a consequence of their multiple realizability, is just what makes cognitive science possible—a scientific investigation of cognitive properties *as such*, across the diverse biological species and perhaps nonbiological cognitive systems, independently of the particulars of their physical implementation. In fact some have even speculated about the possibility of nonphysical realizations of psychologies; it is a seductive thought that there may be contingent empirical laws of cognition, or psychology, that are valid for *cognizers as such*, whether they are protein-based biological organisms like us and other earthly creatures, electromechanical robots, noncarbon-based intelligent extraterrestrials, immaterial Cartesian souls, heavenly angels, or even the omniscient one itself! (This surely takes the idea of "rational psychology" too far.) Even when we bring in the materialist constraint of physical realizationism, the idea of universal laws of cognition and psychology, applicable to all nomologically possible physical systems with cognitive capacities, is heady stuff, indeed.[36]

Whether a given physical property P is a realizer of a mental property M depends on the nature of the system in which P is embedded,[37] since in psychology the input-output behavior of the total system is what is of concern, and the causal role that P plays will depend on the makeup ("causal wiring") of the system as a whole. For example, whether or not tissue damage will cause the nociceptive neurons to fire in a given organism obviously depends on the organism's neural organization, and whether or not the firing of these neural fibers will trigger appropriate escape behavior will again depend on the organism's neural and motor systems. So the same property P, when embedded in a different system, may not realize M. Conversely, there may well be functional substitutes for P in the following sense: if for some reason the normal mechanism for instantiating P in an organism turns dysfunctional, another mechanism with appropriate causal capacities may be able to take its place and supply a near-enough realizer of M for that organism.

The status of P as a realizer of M varies along another dimension as well: since P's credentials as M's realizer depend on its causal/nomic relations to other properties, if laws of nature should vary, thereby altering P's causal potential, that could affect P's status as a realizer of M. P realizes M in this and other nomologically similar worlds; however, in worlds in which different laws hold at the level of M's base domain, thereby generating different causal structures in those worlds, P may fail to satisfy the functional specification definitive of M. In such worlds, M may have realizers entirely different from its realizers in this world, or it may have no realizers at all.[38]

Although the realization relation can shift in these ways, it is also important to note its constancy. Once the system's physical constitution and the prevailing laws of nature are fixed, that fixes whether or not P realizes M in that system. That is to say, if P realizes M in system s, then P will realize M in all systems which are subject to the same laws and which are relevantly indiscernible from s—that is, in respect of nomic properties. If, as most of us would accept, the microstructure of a system determines its causal/nomic properties, it follows that with laws held constant, the realization relation remains invariant for systems with similar microstructures.

Physical Realizationism Explains Mind-Body Supervenience

Consider a class S of systems sharing a relevantly similar microstructure. Biological conspecifics may constitute such a class. Suppose that P realizes M in systems of kind S. From the definition of realization, it follows that P is sufficient for M (that is, if a system of kind S instantiates P at t, it instantiates M at t)—in fact, given the nomological constancy just noted of the realization relation, it follows that P is nomologically sufficient for M. Thus, if $\langle P_1, \ldots, P_n \rangle$ is a realization of $\langle M_1, \ldots, M_n \rangle$, in the sense that each P_i is a realizer of M_i, it follows that the Ms are supervenient on the Ps. Physical realizationism therefore entails the supervenience thesis. Given the relativity of the realization relation to prevailing laws, the entailed supervenience thesis has only the force of nomological necessity, not that of full metaphysical or logical/conceptual necessity. Thus physically indiscernible systems in worlds with different laws may not instantiate the same psychology.

This means that physical realizationism would give us an explanation of the supervenience thesis: the mental supervenes on the physical because mental properties are second-order functional properties with physical realizers (and no nonphysical realizers). And we have an explanation of mental-physical correlations. Why is it that whenever P is realized in a system s, it instantiates mental property M? The answer is that by definition, having M is having a property with causal specification D, and in systems like s, P is the property (or one of the properties) meeting specification D. For systems like s, then, having M *consists in* having P. It isn't that when certain systems instantiate P, mental property M magically emerges or supervenes (in the dictionary sense of "supervene"). It is rather that having M for these systems, simply *is* having P. We might even say, using a familiar if shopworn reductive idiom, that having M, for these systems, is "nothing over and above" having P. Note that all of these explanations are nomological explanations—they depend on the fact that a certain set of laws prevail in our world, for these laws ultimately determine what physical properties are realizers of a given mental property. From a metaphysical point of view, therefore, the idea that mental properties are realized by physical properties goes considerably beyond such ideas as that mental properties have "physical correlates" or "neural substrates," that they have "physical supervenience bases," and the like; unlike "realization," these ideas are not capable of generating an explanation of why a given mental property arises out of, or correlates with, certain physical properties, and do not warrant reductive talk like "Having M, for appropriate systems, *consists in*, or *just is*, having P."

These considerations, I believe, point to a conception of reduction that accords well with the paradigm of reduction in science. To reduce a property, or phenomenon, we first construe it—or reconstrue it—functionally, in terms of its causal/nomic rela-

tions to other properties and phenomena. To reduce temperature, we must first stop thinking of it as an intrinsic property but
construe it as an extrinsic property characterized relationally, in
terms of causal/nomic relations, perhaps something like this: it
is that magnitude of an object that increases (or is caused to
increase) when the object is in contact with another with a higher
degree of it, that, when high, causes a ball of wax in the vicinity
to melt, that causes the sensation of warmth or cold in humans,
that, when extremely low, can make steel brittle, that, when
extremely high, can turn steel into a molten state—you get the
idea. Here is another example: the gene is that mechanism in a
biological organism causally responsible for the transmission of
heritable characteristics from parents to offsprings. To be transparent is to have the kind of molecular structure that causes light
to pass through intact. And so on. We then find properties or
mechanisms, often at the microlevel, that satisfy these causal/
nomic specifications and thereby fill the specified causal roles.
Multiple realization and nomic relativity obtain in these cases as
well. Temperature may be one thing in gases but something else
in solids, plasmas, and vacuums. The DNA molecule is the realizer of the gene, but in worlds in which different basic laws
prevail molecules of another kind may perform the causal functions definitive of the gene. Reductions therefore are doubly
relative: in systems with different structures, the underlying
mechanisms realizing the reduced property may vary, and reductions remain valid only when the basic laws of nature are
held constant—that is, only for nomologically possible worlds
(relative to the reference world).[39]

What has just been described differs in important ways from
the standard model of theory reduction that has dominated the
discussion of reduction, in particular, the possibility of mind-
body reduction. This is Ernest Nagel's model of intertheoretic
reduction whose principal focus is the derivation of laws.[40] According to Nagel, reduction is basically a proof procedure, consisting in the logical-mathematical derivation of the laws of the
target theory from those of the base theory, taken in conjunction
with "bridge laws" connecting the predicates of the two theories.

Standardly, these correlating bridge laws are taken to be biconditional in form, providing each property in the domain of the theory to be reduced with a nomologically coextensive property in the reduction base. For mind-body reduction Nagel's model requires that each mental property be provided with a nomologically coextensive physical property, across all species and structure types. This has made mind-body reductionism—in fact all reductionisms—an easy target. As everyone knows, the most influential antireductionist argument, one that had a decisive role in starting off the antireductionist bandwagon which is still going strong, is based on the claim that on account of the multiple realizability of mental properties, mental properties fail to have coextensions in the physical domain, thereby making mind-body bridge laws unavailable for Nagelian reduction. This argument was then generalized in defense of a general antireductionist position in regard to all special sciences.[41] For three decades the battle over reductionisms has been fought on the question whether or not appropriate bridge laws are available for the domains involved.

But this is the wrong battlefield on which to contest the issue of reduction. What has gone largely unappreciated is the fact that the Nagel model of reduction is in effect the Hempelian D-N model of scientific explanation applied to intertheoretic contexts. Just as Hempelian explanation consists in the derivation of the statement describing the phenomenon to be explained from laws taken together with auxiliary premises describing relevant initial conditions, Nagelian reduction is accomplished in the derivation of the target theory from the base theory taken in conjunction with bridge laws as auxiliary premises. It is therefore more than a little surprising that while the D-N model of explanation has had few committed adherents for over three decades, Nagel's derivational model of reduction is still serving as the dominant standard in discussions of reduction and reductionism.[42] I believe that Nagelian uniform reductions based on universal biconditional bridge laws are extremely rare (if any exists) in the sciences[43]—especially, in the case of microreductions—and that the kind of model adumbrated above is not only more realistic but also, as we will see in a later lecture, more appropriate from a metaphysical point of view. If this is right, the reducibility of a property critically depends on its *functionalizability*—whether or not it can be construed as a second-order functional property over properties in the base domain—not on the availability of bridge laws. Bridge laws are neither necessary nor sufficient for reduction.

We will later take up this and related questions, in connection with mind-body reduction and reductionism (chapter 4). Today I have tried to set the stage for more detailed discussion of some central issues that make up the mind-body problem, in particular the problems of mental causation and mind-body reduction. But several things have become clear: (1) if we are to understand the mind-body relation, we need a positive explanatory account of how mental properties are related to physical properties; (2) Davidson's anomalous monism fails to do this, and likewise with any other similar form of "token physicalism;" (3) even when mind-body supervenience is invoked, that does not help to generate such an account, for the supervenience itself is in need of an explanation; and (4) physical realizationism, whether or not it is ultimately correct, does promise such an account—at least, it has the right form and content. In particular, it can yield an explanation of mind-body supervenience and points to a more realistic model of reduction in terms of which the issue of mind-body reductionism can be more fruitfully debated.

Chapter 2

The Many Problems of Mental Causation

Giving an account of mental causation—in particular, explaining how it is possible for the mental to exercise causal influences in the physical world—has been one of the main preoccupations in the philosophy of mind over the past two decades. The problem of course is not new: as we learn early in our philosophy classes, Descartes was confronted forcefully by his contemporaries on this issue,[1] to explain how there could be causal transactions between minds and bodies. But this does not mean that Descartes's problem is our problem. His problem, as his contemporaries saw, was to show just how his all-too-commonsensical thesis of mind-body interaction was tenable within his ontology of two radically diverse domains of substances, minds and bodies. In his replies, Descartes hemmed and hawed, and was ultimately unable to produce an effective response. Many of his contemporaries, like Leibniz and Malebranche, chose to abandon mental causation in favor of substantival dualism. In staying with mental causation to the end, however, Descartes showed a healthy and commendable respect for philosophical commonsense—more so than many of his major philosophical rivals who opted for radical and implausible solutions—and I believe we should remember him for this as well as for his much publicized failure to reconcile mental causation with his ontology. In any case substance dualism is not the source of our current worries about mental causation; substantival minds are no longer a live philosophical option for most of us.

Philosophical problems do not arise in a vacuum. Typically they emerge when we come to see a conflict among the assumptions and presumptions that we explicitly or tacitly accept, or commitments that command our presumptive respect. The seriousness of a philosophical problem therefore depends on two related questions: First, how deep is our attachment to the assumptions and commitments that give rise to the apparent conflict? Second, how easy or difficult is it to bring the conflicting assumptions into an acceptable reconciliation? The process of reconciliation may require serious modifications to our original commitments. Short of abandoning the entire framework of the existing commitments, compromises must be negotiated. There are no free lunches in philosophy any more than in real life.

In this lecture I want to set out, in what to my mind is the simplest and starkest way, how our principal current problem of mental causation arises. In saying this, I do not want to imply that there is a single problem of mental causation. In fact, as we will shortly see, several different sets of assumptions and principles that many of us find plausible can make trouble for mental causation. I will first describe three sources that seem to generate difficulties for mental causation. This means that we are faced with at least three distinct problems of mental causation. However, in the rest of this lecture, I will focus on one particular version of the third of these problems ("the exclusion problem"). This problem arises from what I will call "the supervenience argument." This, I claim, is our principal problem of mental causation. In referring to this as "our" problem of mental causation, what I mean to suggest is that it is a problem that arises for anyone with the kind of broadly physicalist outlook that many philosophers, including myself, find compelling or, at least, plausible and attractive. In contrast, the other two problems (the mental anomaly problem and the extrinsicness problem) are not essentially tied to physicalism. They are largely independent of physicalist commitments and can arise outside the physicalist framework. As we will see, the exclusion problem is distinctive in that it strikes at the very heart of physicalism, and I believe that the supervenience argument captures the essence of the difficulties involved. The fundamental problem of mental causation for us, then, is to answer this question: How is it possible for the mind to exercise its causal powers in a world that is fundamentally physical?

Let me begin with some reasons for wanting to save mental causation—why it is important to us that mental causation is real (some will say that its existence is an ultimate, nonnegotiable commitment). First, the possibility of human agency evidently requires that our mental states—our beliefs, desires, and intentions—have causal effects in the physical world: in voluntary actions our beliefs and desires, or intentions and decisions, must somehow cause our limbs to move in appropriate ways, thereby causing the objects around us to be rearranged. That is how we manage to cope with our surroundings, write philosophy papers, build bridges and cities, and make holes in the ozone layers. Second, the possibility of human knowledge presupposes the reality of mental causation: perception, our sole window on the world, requires the causation of perceptual experiences and beliefs by physical objects and events around us. Reasoning, by which we acquire new knowledge and belief from the existing fund of what we already know or believe, involves the causation of new belief by old belief; more generally, causation arguably is essential to the transmission of evidential groundedness. Memory is a complex causal process involving interactions between experiences, their physical storage, and retrieval in the form of belief. If you take away perception, memory, and reasoning, you pretty much take away all of human knowledge. To move on, it seems plain that the possibility of psychology as a theoretical science capable of generating law-based explanations of human behavior depends on the reality of mental causation: mental phenomena must be capable of functioning as indispensable links in causal chains leading to physical behavior. A science that invokes mental phenomena in its explanations is presumptively committed to their causal efficacy; for any phenomenon to have an explanatory role, its presence or absence in a given situation must make a difference—a *causal difference.*

It is no wonder then that for most philosophers the causal efficacy of the mental is something that absolutely cannot be given away no matter how great the pressures are from other quarters. Jerry Fodor is among these philosophers; he writes:

> . . . if it isn't literally true that my wanting is causally re-
> sponsible for my reaching, and my itching is causally re-
> sponsible for my scratching, and my believing is causally
> responsible for my saying . . . , if none of that is literally
> true, then practically everything I believe about anything
> is false and it's the end of the world.[2]

If mental causation is only an illusion, that perhaps is not the
end of the world, but it surely seems like the end of a world
that includes Fodor and the rest of us as agents and cognizers.
The problem of determinism threatens human agency, and the
challenge of skepticism threatens human knowledge. The stakes
seem even higher with the problem of mental causation, for this
problem threatens to take away both agency and cognition.

Three Problems of Mental Causation

What then are the assumptions and presumptions that make
trouble for mental causation, prompting us to attempt its "vindication"? I believe there are three doctrines currently on the
scene each of which poses prima facie difficulties for mental
causation. The first two have been with us for some time; the
third, though not new, has begun to receive serious new considerations. One is "mental anomalism," the claim that there are
no causal laws about psychological phenomena. The second
source of the problem is computationalism and content externalism. The third I call "causal exclusion." Each of these generates a distinct problem of mental causation, though the
problems are to some extent interconnected. A truly comprehensive theory of mental causation must provide a solution to each
problem, a solution that simultaneously satisfies the demands
of all three problems.

The Problem of Anomalous Mental Properties

Let us begin with mental anomalism. Davidson's version of this
doctrine holds that there are no causal laws (or, in Davidson's
terms, "strict" laws) about psychological phenomena—no such

laws connecting mental events with physical events and no such laws connecting mental events with other mental events.[3] But why does mental anomalism pose a difficulty for mental causation? The initial difficulty arises when anomalism is combined with the widely accepted nomological requirement on causal relations,[4] the condition that events standing in a causal relation must instantiate a causal law. But this seems to make mental causation impossible: mental causation requires mental events to instantiate laws, but mental anomalism says there are no laws about mental events.

Davidson's own proposal is well-known; he calls it "anomalous monism." We have already considered it as a mind-body theory and found it wanting (chapter 1); but here our interest lies in Davidson's ingenious argument leading to his physical monism. True, says Davidson, mental events in causal relations must instantiate laws but since there aren't any psychological laws, that can only mean that they instantiate physical laws. This shows that mental events fall under physical kinds (or have true physical descriptions), from which it further follows, argues Davidson, that they are physical events. This is the monism in his anomalous monism. The general upshot of the argument is that for any event to enter into a causal relation, it must be covered by a physical law and hence be part of the physical domain. Causal relations can obtain only between physical events covered by physical laws, although of course some of these events are also mental events. The causal structure of this world—the total set of causal relations that hold in this world—is entirely due to the prevailing physical laws. Mental events are causally efficacious therefore only because they are identical with causally efficacious physical events.

But this ingenious solution has failed to satisfy very many philosophers. On the contrary, there has been an impressive unanimity among Davidson's commentators on just why anomalous monism falls short as an account of mental causation.[5] Take any mental event m that stands in a causal relation, say as a cause of event e. According to Davidson, this causal relation obtains just in case m and e instantiate a physical law.

Thus m falls under a certain physical (perhaps, neural) kind N, e falls under a physical kind P, and an appropriate causal law connects events of kind N with events of kind P. But this apparently threatens the causal relevance of mentality: the fact that m is a mental event—that it is the kind of mental event it is— appears to have no role in determining what causal relations it enters into. Event m's causal relations are fixed, wholly and exclusively, by the totality of its physical properties, and there is in this picture no causal work that m's mental properties can, or need to, contribute.[6] If mental properties were arbitrarily redistributed over the events of this world, or even if mentality were wholly removed from this world—possibilities apparently left open by Davidson's mental anomalism—that would not affect a single causal relation between events of this world, leaving the causal structure of the world entirely untouched. This seems to consign mental properties to the status of epiphenomena.[7] Thus the problem of mental causation arising out of mental anomalism is to answer this question: *How can anomalous properties be causal properties?* A solution to this problem would have to show either that contrary to Davidson, mental properties are not in reality anomalous, or that being anomalous in Davidson's sense is no barrier to their having causal relevance or being causally efficacious.

There have been several attempts to rehabilitate the causal status of mental properties within the constraint of mental anomalism. Most of these attempts have taken the tack of relaxing, or somehow circumventing, the nomological requirement on causal relations. This is usually done in one of three ways. First, you may want to allow laws that are less than "strict," perhaps laws tacitly qualified by "ceteris paribus" clauses, to subsume individual events in causal relations, and argue that there are nonstrict laws of this kind involving mental properties. Second, you look to some form of counterfactual dependency, rather than subsumptive causal laws, to generate causal relations. Fodor's approach[8] is an example of the first strategy; those of LePore and Loewer's[9] and of Horgan's[10] are examples of the second. A third approach (which is consistent with the second) is to define a notion of causal relevance or efficacy weaker than causation regulated by strict laws. A version of this approach, recently embraced by Davidson,[11] attempts to invoke supervenience of the mental on the physical to explain the causal relevance of the mental. But, as we will see, mind-body supervenience itself can be seen to lead to difficulties for mental causation.

The Problem of Extrinsic Mental Properties
Let us begin with syntacticalism, the view that only "syntactic" properties of mental states, not their "semantic" (or "content" or "representational") properties, can be causally relevant—in particular, to behavior causation.[12] Given the further assumption that the mentality of an important class of mental states, like beliefs and desires, consists in their semantic or representational character, syntacticalism appears to force upon us the conclusion that the intentional properties of mental states, the properties that are constitutive of their mentality, are causally irrelevant. But what persuades us to take syntacticalism seriously?

Syntacticalism most naturally arises in the context of computationalism, an approach that urges us to view mental processes as computational processes on internal representations, on the model of information processing in digital computers. It is apparent that computational processes—that is, causal processes that constitute computation—are sensitive to the syntax, not semantics, of the representations or data structures that are being manipulated; it is the shapes, not meanings, of symbols that determine the course of computation. It matters none to computation whether a given string of 1s and 0s means the inventory count of toothpaste at the local supermarket, the atmospheric pressure in Providence at noon today, the altitude of an airplane on a landing approach, or nothing at all. Similarly, if mental activities are computational processes on beliefs, desires, and such, it would seem that it is the syntactic shapes of these states, not their representational contents, that are causally relevant.[13]

The essential problem here is easily divorced from computationalism and talk of an inner mental language with a syntax and semantics. The internal cause of physical behavior must be supervenient on the total internal state of the agent or organism at the time.[14] For it seems highly plausible to assume that if two organisms are in an identical total internal state at a given time, they will emit identical motor output. However, semantic properties of internal states are not in general supervenient on their *synchronous internal* properties, for as a rule they involve facts about the organism's history and ecological conditions.[15] Thus two organisms whose total states at a given time have identical intrinsic properties can differ in respect of the semantical properties they instantiate; they can differ in the contents of their beliefs and desires, the extensions of their homophonic predicates, and the truth conditions of their homophonic sentences. But prima facie these semantical differences should make no difference to behavior output. The realization that ordinary content ascriptions have this extrinsic/relational dimension is one of the more notable developments in the philosophy of mind and language during the past two decades.[16] You on this earth have the belief that water is wet; yet, as the story goes, your exact physical duplicate on Twin Earth believes that XYZ is wet, not that water is wet. Frogs on the earth, when appropriately stimulated optically, have the "belief" that a fly is flitting across its visual field (or, at any rate, "sees" a fly); frogs on another planet without flies, when identically stimulated, don't have a belief about flies, or at any rate are not in a state that represent flies— they "believe" that a "schmy" is flitting across its visual field (schmies are tiny black bats which the frogs of this other planet feed on). Thus, that a given intentional state of an organism instantiates a certain semantic property is a *relational* fact, a fact that essentially involves the organism's relationship to various external environmental and historical factors. This makes semantic properties relational, or extrinsic, whereas we expect causative properties involved in behavior production to be non-relational, or intrinsic, properties of the organism. If inner states are implicated in behavior causation, it seems that all the causal work is done by their "syntactic," or at any rate internal/intrinsic, properties, leaving their semantic properties causally otiose. The problem of mental causation generated by syntacticalism therefore is to answer the following question: *How can extrinsic, relational properties be causally efficacious in behavior production?*

So the crux of the problem lies in the supposed fact that mental properties, in particular, content properties (e.g., being a belief that P), are relational properties, extrinsic to the organisms instantiating them, whereas we expect the causative properties of behavior to be intrinsic and internal.[17]

The Problem of Causal Exclusion
The third, and final, problem about mental causation I have in mind arises as follows: suppose that we have somehow put together an account of how mental events can be causes of physical events, an account that meets the requirements of the problems of anomalous mental properties and of syntacticalism. Suppose then that mental event m, occurring at time t, causes physical event p, and let us suppose that this causal relation holds in virtue of the fact that m is an event of mental kind M and p an event of physical kind P. Does p also have a physical cause at t, an event of some physical kind N?

To acknowledge mental event m (occurring at t) as a cause of physical event p but deny that p has a physical cause at t would be a clear violation of the causal closure of the physical domain, a relapse into Cartesian interactionist dualism which mixes physical and nonphysical events in a single causal chain. But to acknowledge that p has also a physical cause, p^*, at t is to invite the question: Given that p has a physical cause p^*, what causal work is left for m to contribute? The physical cause therefore threatens to exclude, and preempt, the mental cause. This is the problem of causal exclusion. The antireductive physicalist who wants to remain a mental realist, therefore, must give an account of how the mental cause and the physical cause of one and the same event are related to each other. Token physicalism, like Davidson's anomalous monism, is not enough, since the question ultimately involves the causal efficacy of mental *properties,* and antireductionism precludes their reductive identification with physical properties. Thus the problem of causal exclusion is to answer this question: *Given that every physical event that has a cause has a physical cause, how is a mental cause also possible?*

These then are the three principal ways in which I believe the problem of mental causation arises in current debates in philosophy of mind. This means that there really are three separable problems, although of course this does not preclude their resolution by a single unified approach. Here I will not deal directly with the first two problems; as I said at the outset of this talk, what I want to do is to develop the third problem—the exclusion problem—in a more concrete and detailed way by focusing on the two theses we discussed in my first lecture, namely the claim that the mental supervenes on the physical and the claim that the mental is realized in the physical. I hope to show how both mind-body supervenience and physical realizationism can be seen to lead to prima facie difficulties for mental causation. In a later lecture I will discuss how physical realizationism, via a functional reduction of mental properties, presents an opening for a possible accommodation of mentality within the causal structure of the physical world, although the opening may well turn out to be not wide enough to let in all mental properties.

The Supervenience Argument, or Descartes's Revenge

In my first lecture I argued that mind-body supervenience could usefully be thought of as defining minimal physicalism—that it is the minimal commitment that anyone who calls herself a physicalist should be willing to accept. We saw also that mind-body supervenience is entailed by physical realizationism, the thesis that mental properties are instantiated in virtue of being realized by physical properties in physical systems. Moreover emergentism, too, is arguably committed to mind-body supervenience: if two systems are wholly alike physically, we should expect the same mental properties to emerge, or fail to emerge, in each.

Let us now turn to an argument designed to show that mind-body supervenience itself leads to apparent difficulties with mental causation. If we take the supervenience thesis to define minimal physicalism, as I earlier suggested, the argument will show that these difficulties will beset physicalism in general—that is, even the weakest form of physicalism must come to terms with this argument one way or another. If this is right, abandoning the substantival dualism of Descartes doesn't get us out of the woods as far as mental causation is concerned. Indeed one notable development in the recent philosophy of mind is the return of the problem of mental causation as a serious challenge to mainstream physicalism, a phenomenon that would have amused Descartes.

I will now proceed to construct a dilemma-style argument that apparently leads to the conclusion that mental causation is unintelligible. In essence the argument to be presented is the result of superimposing mind-body supervenience on the causal exclusion problem. We begin by setting forth the two horns of the dilemma:

(i) Either mind-body supervenience holds or it fails.

But what does mind-body supervenience assert? Let me restate the mind-body supervenience thesis:

Mind-body supervenience Mental properties supervene on physical properties in the sense that if something instantiates any mental property M at t, there is a physical base property P such that the thing has P at t, and necessarily anything with P at a time has M at that time.

Note that a base property is *necessarily* sufficient for the supervenient property; the necessity involved here is standardly taken to be at least *nomological necessity*—so that if mind-body supervenience holds, it holds in all worlds that share with our world the same fundamental laws of nature.

Returning to (i), we briefly pursue the second horn first:

(ii) If mind-body supervenience fails, there is no visible
way of understanding the possibility of mental causation.

According to Jerry Fodor, "If mind/body supervenience goes,
the intelligibility of mental causation goes with it."[18] To my
knowledge he has never explained why he has said this (and
not just once!). Fodor is not alone in tying the fate of mental
causation to supervenience: Horgan, for example, has argued
for the physical supervenience of qualia on the ground that it
is needed to make qualia causally efficacious.[19] But what exactly
is the connection between supervenience and mental causation?
The simplest and most obvious reason for the physicalist to
accept (ii) lies, I think, in her commitment to *the causal closure
of the physical domain,* an idea that has already made a brief
appearance above. One way of stating the principle of physical
causal closure is this: If you pick any physical event and trace
out its causal ancestry or posterity, that will never take you
outside the physical domain. That is, no causal chain will ever
cross the boundary between the physical and the nonphysical.
The interactionist dualism of Descartes is in clear contravention
of this principle. If you reject this principle, you are ipso facto
rejecting the in-principle completability of physics—that is, the
possibility of a complete and comprehensive physical theory of
all physical phenomena. For you would be saying that any
complete explanatory theory of the physical domain must invoke nonphysical causal agents. Never mind a complete physical explanation of everything there is; there couldn't even be a
complete physical explanation of everything physical. It is safe
to assume that no serious physicalist could accept such a
prospect.

Now if mind-body supervenience fails—that is, if the mental
domain floats freely, unanchored in the physical domain, causation from the mental to the physical would obviously breach the
physical causal closure. Mind-body supervenience grounds each
mental phenomenon in the physical domain by providing for it
a set of physical conditions that are (at least) nomologically
sufficient for it and on which its occurrence depends. A corollary

is the thesis that no mental phenomenon can occur, and no mental property can be instantiated, unless an appropriate physical base condition is present. Every mental event, be it a sensation like pain or itch, or an intentional state like belief and desire, must have a physical basis: it occurs because an appropriate physical basis is present, and it would not occur if such a basis was absent.[20] These comments hold true if you wish to speak in terms of realization. If any mental property gets instantiated because, and only because, one of its physical realizers is instantiated, there is a similar dependence of mental occurrences on physical occurrences.

In any case mind-body supervenience brings mental phenomena within the ambit of the physical: the physical determines the mental, and in that sense the mental does not constitute an ontologically independent domain that injects causal influences into the physical domain from the outside. Now it is another question whether or not mind-body supervenience brings the mental *close enough* to the physical to allow mental causation to circumvent the constraint of the physical causal closure.[21] But we can skirt this question here, for if the answer is no, that would only show that mind-body supervenience isn't enough to give us a solution to the problem of causal exclusion of the mental by the physical. But there is a potentially more serious problem with supervenience: mind-body supervenience may itself be a source of the problem. That is, mind-body supervenience, far from being part of the solution, as hoped for by Fodor, Horgan, and others, may turn out to be part of the problem. Let us now look into this possibility.

> (iii) Suppose that an instance of mental property M causes another mental property M^* to be instantiated.

So this is a case of mental-to-mental causation, one in which an instance of a mental property causes an instance of another mental property. We may take "instances" or "instantiations" of properties as events, states, or phenomena. For brevity, I will often speak of one property causing another property; this is to be understood to mean that an *instance* of the first causes an *instance* of the second.[22] Returning to our argument, we see that (ii), the supervenience premise, yields:

(iv) M^* has a physical supervenience base P^*.

We now ask the following critical question: *Where does this instance of M^* come from? How does M^* get instantiated on this occasion?* There apparently are two possible answers to consider:

(v) M^* is instantiated on this occasion: (a) because, ex hypothesi, M caused M^* to be instantiated; (b) because P^*, the physical supervenience base of M^*, is instantiated on this occasion.

I hope that you are like me in seeing a real tension between these two answers: Under the assumption of mind-body supervenience, M^* occurs because its supervenience base P^* occurs, and as long as P^* occurs, M^* must occur no matter what other events preceded this instance of M^*—in particular, regardless of whether or not an instance of M preceded it. This puts the claim of M to be a cause of M^* in jeopardy: P^* alone seems fully responsible for, and capable of accounting for, the occurrence of M^*.[23] As long as P^*, or another base property of M^*, is present, that absolutely guarantees the presence of M^*, and unless such a base is there on this occasion, M^* can't be there either. Given this, the only way anything can have a role in the causation of M^* would have to be via its relationship to M^*'s supervenience base P^*, and as far as I can see, the only way of reconciling the claim of M to be a cause of M^* with the fact that M^* has P^* as its supervenience base is to accept this:

(vi) M caused M^* *by causing* P^*. That is how this instance of M caused M^* to be instantiated on this occasion.

There may be a plausible general principle involved here, which is by itself sufficient to justify (vi) even if you do not see the tension in (v), and it is this: *To cause a supervenient property to be instantiated, you must cause its base property (or one of its base properties) to be instantiated.* To relieve a headache, you take aspirin: that is, you causally intervene in the brain process on which the headache supervenes. That's the only way we can do anything about our headaches. To make your painting more beautiful, more expressive, or more dramatic, you must do physical work on the painting and thereby alter the physical supervenience base of the aesthetic properties you want to improve. There is no direct way of making your painting more beautiful or less beautiful; you must change it physically if you want to change it aesthetically—there is no other way.

But note what (vi) asserts: it says that a mental property M causes a physical property P^* to be instantiated. This of course is a case of mental-to-physical causation. So what our argument has shown so far is this: *Under the mind-body supervenience assumption, mental-to-mental causation implies, or presupposes, mental-to-physical causation.* So the question that we now face is whether we can make sense of mental-to-physical causation—that is, under the premise of mind-body supervenience.[24]

Going back to (vi): we see that on the assumption of mind-body supervenience, it follows:

(vii) M itself has a physical supervenience base P.

We must now compare M and P in regard to their causal status with respect to P^*. When we reflect on this point, I believe, we begin to see reasons for taking P as preempting the claim of M as a cause of P^*. If you take causation as grounded in nomological sufficiency, P qualifies as a cause of P^*, for, since P is sufficient for M and M is sufficient for P^*, P is sufficient for P^*. If you choose to understand causation in terms of counterfactuals, again there is good reason to think that P qualifies: if P hadn't occurred M would not have occurred (we may assume, without prejudice, that no alternative physical base of M would have been available on this occasion), and given that if M had not occurred P^* would not have occurred, we may reasonably conclude that if P had not occurred, P^* would not have either.[25]

It seems then that we are now blessed with an overabundance of causes: both M and P seem severally eligible as a sufficient cause of P^*. And it is not possible to escape the threat of causal overdetermination by thinking of the situation as involving a causal chain from P to M and then to P^*, with M as an intermediate causal link. For the relation from P to M is not happily thought of as a causal relation; in general, the relation between base properties and supervenient properties is not happily construed as causal.[26] For one thing, the instantiations of the related properties are wholly simultaneous, whereas causes are standardly thought to precede their effects; second, it is difficult, perhaps incoherent, to imagine a causal chain, with intermediate links, between the subvenient and the supervenient properties. What intermediate stages could link the beauty of a painting to its physical properties? What intermediary events could causally connect a mental event with its subvenient physical base? Would such intermediaries themselves be mental or physical? Moreover, for the present case, the causal chain approach, in taking M to be a nonphysical cause of P^*, would violate the causal closure of the physical domain, an option foreclosed to the physicalist.

Nor does it seem plausible to take M and P together to constitute a single sufficient cause of P^*. There are two reasons for this. First, P alone is causally sufficient for P^*, and so is M. It is difficult to see how M and P together can pack any more causal power than M alone or P alone. Second, this approach is plausible only if it claims M to be a necessary component in the causation of P^*, and this means that, as with the causal chain proposal, it involves a violation of the physical causal closure. For a complete causal explanation of why P^* was instantiated on this occasion would have to advert to the presence of a nonphysical causal agent, M, in addition to P.

And, finally, it is not possible to take this simply as a case of causal overdetermination—that the instance of P^* is causally overdetermined by two sufficient causes, P and M. Apart from the implausible consequence that it makes every case of mental causation a case of overdetermination, this approach encounters two difficulties: first, in making a physical cause available to substitute for every mental cause, it appears to make mental causes dispensable in any case; second, the approach may come into conflict with the physical causal closure. For consider a world in which the physical cause does not occur and which in other respects is as much like our world as possible. The over-determination approach says that in such a world, the mental cause causes a physical event—namely that the principle of causal closure of the physical domain no longer holds. I do not think we can accept this consequence: that a minimal counter-factual supposition like that can lead to a major change in the world.

It seems to me that the most natural way of viewing the situation is this:

(viii) P caused P^*, and M supervenes on P and M^* super-venes on P^*.

This explains the observed regularities between M-instances and M^*-instances, and those between M-instances and P^*-instances.[27] These regularities are by no means accidental; in a clear sense they are law-based, and may even be able to support appropriate counterfactuals. However, if we understand the difference between genuine, productive and generative causal processes, on the one hand, and the noncausal regularities that are observed because they are parasitic on real causal processes, we are in a position to understand the picture recommended by (viii). In the case of supposed M-M^* causation, the situation is rather like a series of shadows cast by a moving car: there is no causal connection between the shadow of the car at one instant and its shadow an instant later, each being an effect of the moving car. The moving car represents a genuine causal proc-ess, but the series of shadows it casts, however regular and lawlike it may be, does not constitute a causal process.[28] Hence we have:

(ix) The M-to-M^* and M-to-P^* causal relations are only apparent, arising out of a genuine causal process from P to P^*.

Whence a dilemma:

> (x) If mind-body supervenience fails, mental causation is unintelligible; if it holds, mental causation is again unintelligible. Hence mental causation is unintelligible.

That then is the supervenience argument against mental causation, or Descartes's revenge against the physicalists. I believe it poses a serious challenge to physicalism by casting doubts on the possibility of mental causation within the parameters it sets for itself. Descartes's difficulties arose from the duality of mental and material substances. Current mainstream physicalism, which calls itself "nonreductive physicalism," runs into parallel difficulties on account of its commitment to the duality of psychological and physical properties—or its failure to make a reductionist commitment for psychological properties. For it is clear that the tacit assumption that gets the supervenience argument going is mind-body antireductionism; if the mental properties are viewed as reducible to physical properties in an appropriate way, we should expect to be able to disarm the argument (although of course the details will need to be worked out).

One good question to raise about the foregoing argument is this: Wouldn't the same argument show that all properties that supervene on basic physical properties are epiphenomenal, and that their causal efficacy is unintelligible? However, there seems to be more than ample reason to think that geological properties, say, are supervenient on fundamental physical properties, and if mind-body supervenience could be shown to put mental causation in jeopardy, wouldn't the very same considerations do the same for geological properties? But no one seems to worry about geological causation, and there evidently seems no reason to start worrying. If so, shouldn't we conclude that there must be something wrong with the argument of the preceding section?[29]

I will deal with this question in detail in my two remaining lectures. As I see it, however, the heart of the issue here is this: with properties like geological and biological properties, we are much more willing, intuitively, to accept a reductionist picture in relation to basic physical properties. I believe that this is true even for philosophers who are vocal in their claim that anti-reductionism holds across the board, at all levels in relation to their lower levels, and that geological and biological properties are no more reducible to basic physical properties than mental properties. Clearly it is possible that their antireductionism is more correct about mental properties than about these other "higher-level" physical properties.

We will take up the reductionist way out in a later lecture. Let us now turn to a consideration of some real-life philosophical positions that appear to be directly vulnerable to the argument we have constructed.

Searle, Fodor, and the Supervenience Argument

I now want to show that the recent proposals by two well-known philosophers of mind apparently succumb to the supervenience argument. In *The Rediscovery of Mind*[30] John Searle argues for a position he calls "biological naturalism." Broadly, it is the view that mental phenomena, with all their subjectivity and qualitative character, are natural biological phenomena, no different in principle from phenomena of digestion or reproduction. In particular, Searle maintains that mental phenomena are *caused* by biological phenomena, presumably neural processes in the brain, and that this makes them "features of the brain." Although Searle sometimes makes use of the idioms of "supervenience" and "emergence," he gives them highly idiosyncratic causal readings, and it is clear that where others would say that mental phenomena supervene on, or emerge from, their underlying neural substrates, Searle would say that they are caused by these lower-level processes.

Searle is a mental realist, and believes in the causal efficacy of the mental—in particular, the causal powers of consciousness. According to him, "consciousness does all sorts of things," and "consciousness enables the organism to act on the world, to produce effects in the world."[31] As just noted, Searle substitutes the causal idiom for the supervenience idiom and would describe the relation between a mental property and its underlying neural correlate in terms of causation rather than supervenience or emergence (in their standard senses). However, it is not difficult to see that this does not enable Searle to escape the dilemma posed by the supervenience argument. Suppose that an instance of a mental property, M, causes another mental property, M^*, to be instantiated—an instance of "going left to right from macro to macro" as Searle calls it[32] (this corresponds to step (iii) in the supervenience argument). According to Searle's biological naturalism, every mental phenomenon is caused by a neurobiological phenomenon, and this means that this instance of M^* is caused by (an instance of) a neural property P^* (step (iv)). We now must ask: Where does this instance of M^* come from? How does M^* get instantiated on this occasion?

And again we get two answers: (1) ex hypothesi, M^* was caused to be instantiated by M, and (2) according to Searle's biological naturalism, M^* was caused to be instantiated by neural property P^*. It looks as though the instantiation of M^* is causally overdetermined, and this generalizes to all mental phenomena. We are clearly in need of a plausible story that reconciles (1) and (2) without making every case of mental-to-mental causation an instance of causal overdetermination. From here on we can run the same argument, with little alteration, that we developed earlier.

To arguments of this kind Searle has responded as follows:[33]

> Does this imply overdetermination? Not at all. The same system is being described at different levels. . . . In short, the same system admits of different causal descriptions at different levels all of which are consistent and none of which implies either overdetermination or failure of causal closure.

> I now, let us suppose, have a conscious feeling of pain. This is caused by patterns of neuron firings and is realized in the system of neurons. Suppose the pain causes a desire to take an aspirin. The desire is also caused by patterns of

neuron firings and is realized in the system of neurons. . . .
I can truly say both that my pain caused my desire and that
sequences of neuron firings caused other sequences. These
are two different but consistent descriptions of the same
system given at different levels.

According to Searle then we can affirm, without fear of overdetermination, all of the following: (1) that M (pain) causes M^*
(desire to take aspirin); (2) that P (a sequence of neuron firings)
causes P^* (another sequence of neuron firings); (3) P causes M;
and (4) P^* causes M^*. This is perfectly all right, Searle assures
us, because (1) and (2) are "descriptions of the same system
given at different levels." This certainly is a view one could hold
of the situation; however, what isn't at all clear is whether Searle
can, or should wish to. For saying that "pain causes a desire for
aspirin" and "neural firings P cause neural firings P^*" are _de-
scriptions of the same situation_[34] is plausible only if you are prepared to say that "pain" and "neural firings P" are descriptions
of the same phenomenon (at "different levels"), and similarly
for "desire for aspirin" and "neural firings P^*"—that is, only if
you are willing to say that pain = neural firings P, and that
desire for aspirin = neural firings P^*.

Speaking for myself, I don't think that this is an implausible
move; in fact some form of reductionism of this kind may well
turn out to be the only viable view if mental events are to have
a genuine causal role in the physical world. But let us return to
Searle: it should be clear that psychoneural identities of this kind
put into jeopardy Searle's claim that neural firings P _cause_ the
pain, and that neural firings P^* _cause_ the aspirin desire. If these
causal claims are to stand, "pain" and "neural firings P" can't be
descriptions of the same phenomenon, and similarly for the
other pair. Searle of course says that these descriptions are "at
different levels." But what could that mean? And what difference could that make? Searle needs to come up with a reasonable
ontology and language of causation to make his central claims
about the mind-body relation intelligible and consistent. Also,
and perhaps more important, it is not at all clear how the view

that pain talk and talk of neural firings are about the very same phenomena but only at different levels squares with Searle's doctrine of the "subjective ontology" of the mental and the irreducibility of consciousness. But these are not matters that concern us here.

Let us now turn to Fodor. In a recent paper in which he attempts to defend the causal efficacy of the mental,[35] he writes:

> According to the present view, the properties projected in the laws of basic science are causally responsible, and so too are the properties projected in the laws of the special sciences. . . . Notice, in particular, that even if the properties that the special sciences talk about are supervenient upon the properties that the basic sciences talk about, that does *not* argue that the properties that the special sciences talk about are epiphenomenal.

The burden of the supervenience argument is precisely that the supervenience of the special-science properties on the basic-science properties does in fact argue, at least presumptively, for the conclusion that the special-science properties are threatened by epiphenomenalism. But why is Fodor so confident that we can have it both ways—the supervenience and causal efficacy of special-science properties? The passage quoted above continues as follows:

> Not, at least, if there are causal laws of the special sciences. The causal laws of the special sciences and causal laws of basic sciences have in common that they *both* license ascriptions of causal responsibility.

We can concede to Fodor the claim that there are special-science *laws*—statements of the form "F-events are regularly followed by G-events" with a modal force appropriate for laws, where F and G are properties or kinds in a special science. And these laws may support counterfactuals, serve as predictive instruments, and may even generate serviceable explanations.[36] But whether these are *causal laws*, laws of the form "F-events, in virtue of being instantiations of property F, *cause* G-events," is what is at issue. And this question takes us right back to the supervenience argument; for until the pressure of this argument has satisfactorily been relieved, we are not entitled to interpret special-science laws as causal laws in their own right.

Block's Worries about Second-Order Properties

The red color of the bullfighter's cape provokes the bull (or so the story goes)—that is, it causes the bull to get angry. But is the *provocativeness* of the cape—its "second-order" property of *having some property or other that causes anger*—also a cause of the bull's anger? A certain chemical property of a Seconal pill puts you to sleep. The pill also has *dormitivity*, the second-order property of having some property or other that puts people to sleep; in short, it is a "sleeping pill." Is the dormitivity of the pill itself also a cause of your falling asleep?

In a recent paper,[37] Ned Block worries about such questions, and an examination of these worries, I believe, is a good way of seeing how the realization relation, like the supervenience relation, can lead to problems with mental causation. In any case the reason Block worries about these questions is that he thinks the correct answer to them is no (that is, the provocativeness of the cape is *not* a cause, in addition to its redness, of the bull's anger), and that, on the functionalist conception of mental properties that he favors,[38] mental properties might be in the same boat—they too are second-order properties that consist in the having of some property or other satisfying a certain causal specification. Being in pain, on the functionalist account, is the second-order property of instantiating some property or other, presumably a neurobiological property, that causes wincings, cryings, limb withdrawals, and the like. If so, can pain itself, in addition to its neural realizers, be considered a cause of wincings and cryings?

If Block's worries are well-founded, functionalists are in deep trouble: mental properties would be threatened with the loss of causal powers, and the fact that an event falls under a given mental kind (say, pain) would have nothing to do with what effects it may cause. In short, functionalism might turn out to be a form of epiphenomenalism, and the received ("official") view of cognitive science as an autonomous special science, which generates its own distinctive law-based causal explanations at higher, formal/abstract cognitive levels, faces an imminent collapse. There is irony in the fact that this is precisely the conception of cognitive science that has been inspired and promoted by functionalism—in particular, the view that the properties studied by cognitive science are second-order properties that abstract from the nitty-gritty physical/biological details of the cognitive systems that realize them.

But why does it seem wrong, at least odd, to say that the provocativeness of the cape, in addition to its red color, is a cause of the bull's anger? It seems that Block sees two prima facie reasons, only one of which he decides to take seriously. First, Block's serious reason: for the cape to be provocative (in relation to bulls) is, *by definition,* for it to have a property that causes bulls to get angry. This seems to make the singular causal attribution analytic, or definitionally true, whereas we would expect such attributions to be contingent and empirical. We will return to this point later. Second, the point Block does not in the end take seriously: counting the cape's provocativeness as well as its color as a cause seemingly leads to an overabundance of causes—that is, causal overdetermination. For the bull's anger would have two distinct causes, the cape's color and its provocativeness. (Notice the parallel with the move from (vii) to (viii) in the supervenience argument.)

But why doesn't Block think the multiplicity of causes is a real problem? He says that "we are normally reluctant to accept overdetermination because it is wrong, other things equal, to postulate coincidences."[39] We can agree with Block that, unlike in the paradigmatic cases of causal overdetermination (say, two bullets hitting a person in the heart simultaneously), the cape's having the two properties, redness and provocativeness, is not a case of coincidence (for presumably its provocativeness depends on its being red). But it is not clear why Block thinks that this diffuses the problem. Perhaps, Block's reasoning is that in cases of standard overdetermination, the overdetermining causes are *independent* events—two or more independent causal chains, each causally sufficient, converge upon a single effect. In contrast, in the case of the cape's color and its provocativeness, we do not evidently have two independent causes: the instantiation of provocativeness, as a second-order property, is dependent on the instantiation of the color red. What isn't clear, however, is why this removes the difficulty: if the color of the cape is, in and of itself, a sufficient cause of the anger (at least, sufficient in the circumstance), what *further* causal work is left for its provocativeness? What special contribution of its own can the cape's provocativeness make in the causation of the anger? The answer obviously is none: given the color of the cape as a full cause, there is no *additional* causal work left for its provocativeness, or anything else.[40] It should be clear then that there is a real problem, the exclusion problem, in recognizing second-order properties as causally efficacious in addition to their realizers. This is not surprising, since second-order properties, hence mental properties construed as functional properties, supervene on their first-order realizers. The exclusion problem doesn't go away when we recognize the two purported causes as in some way related to each other, perhaps one being dependent on the other. As long as they are recognized as distinct events, each claiming to be a full cause of a single event, the problem remains. Describing this case as a case of overdetermination perhaps has clouded the issues for Block; perhaps this led him to think that to dissolve the problem it suffices to show that the present case is not a standard case of causal overdetermination. However, our problem is not exactly that of causal overdetermination, although both have to do with an overabundance of causes. It is important to see that the problem that we face arises *because* the two putative causes are *not* independent events. The difficulty is exactly that the causal status of the dependent event is threatened by the event on which it depends. The exclusion problem, therefore, is very much alive with the case of the cape's color and its provocativeness as multiple causes of one and the same event.[41]

For this reason, I believe, Block mislocates the real problem that arises for the causal efficacy of mental properties when they are taken to be second-order properties defined in terms of causal roles. That he takes, erroneously in my view, the analyticity issue as the main difficulty, can be seen in the significant qualification he places on the epiphenomenalism that he believes we must accept. For his epiphenomenalism comes only to this:

> *Block's epiphenomenalism:* A second-order property, defined as the property of *having some property that causes property K*,[42] is epiphenomenal *with respect to K*.

Thus pain, defined as a state apt for causing winces, groans, and escape behavior, cannot be considered as a cause of winces, groans, and escape behavior, but it presumably can have causal effects of other sorts. Block in fact claims that the dormitivity of Seconal, in spite of its admitted impotence to cause sleep, can have effects of other kinds, for it is possible, he says, that there is a law to the effect that dormitivity of a pill is causally sufficient for the ingester's getting cancer.[43] However, as is evident, this could be the case only if each specific chemical realizer of dormitivity caused cancer; it is difficult to see how dormitivity as such, independently of its realizers, can cause cancer or anything else. To generalize, I find the following principle highly plausible (I have elsewhere called it "the causal inheritance principle"[44]):

> If a second-order property F is realized on a given occasion by a first-order property H (that is, if F is instantiated on a given occasion in virtue of the fact that one of its realizers, H, is instantiated on that occasion), then the causal powers of this particular instance of F are identical with (or are a subset of[45]) the causal powers of H (or of this instance of H).

For there is nothing in the instantiation of F on this occasion over and above the instantiation of its realizer H. Given this, to think that this instance of F has causal powers in excess of those of H is tantamount to belief in magic: somehow new causal powers miraculously materialize as we define second-order and higher-order properties from a fixed stock of first-order properties!

Notice that the analyticity issue arises only for functional properties—second-order properties defined by causal specifications—not for all second-order properties. But the exclusion problem—that is, the threat posed by first-order realizers to preempt the causal claims of the second-order properties they realize—is entirely general; it arises for all second-order properties, whether or not they are functional. Block, and the rest of us, have reason to worry about epiphenomenalism for functional mental properties *tout court*, not just in relation to the effects in terms of which they are defined.

How does the supervenience argument presented earlier apply to mental properties construed as functional properties, that is, second-order properties defined by causal specification? It is clear that the argument places the causal efficacy of such properties in jeopardy. For suppose that a given instance of M causes an instance of M^*. On this occasion M^* is realized, let us assume, by first-order physical property P^*. We ask: How did M^* get to be instantiated on this occasion? And again we get two answers: (1) because M caused M^*, and (2) because P^* realized M^*. And this creates an apparent tension, and so forth. But notice that the argument gets appreciably more direct and its impact more salient. For when we try to relieve the said tension by saying that this instance of M caused P^* to be instantiated (thereby causing M^* to be instantiated), we must reflect on what this means in light of the causal inheritance principle. For the principle says that our instance of M inherits all of its causal powers from the first-order property that realizes M on this occasion, and this first-order property is P. So this instance of M can claim to cause the P^*-instance insofar as, and only insofar as, this instance of P causes it. And it becomes entirely unclear what could motivate us to countenance the M-instance, in addition to the P-instance that realizes it, as a cause of the P^* instance.

At this point we are compelled to make some choices. In particular, the pressure to identify the M-instance with the

P-instance is all but irresistible, and there are at least two reasons for this. First, as we saw, the very conception of second-order properties and their realizers strongly incline us to deny that there can be anything to the instantiation of a second-order property over and above the instantiation of one of its realizers. For M to be instantiated on a given occasion *is* for one of its realizers to be instantiated on that occasion, and on this occasion it is P that realizes M. Second, if the causal powers of the M-instance are identical with those of its realizing P-instance, what reasons can we have for thinking there are here two events, not one? On a plausible view of properties,[46] only causally relevant or efficacious properties should count as individuating properties, and it is in any case highly implausible to say that events that are indiscernible in respect of causal properties can yet be distinct events.[47]

This then is one way in which the pressure toward mind-body reductionism is generated. We will on a later occasion examine the issue of reductionism in greater detail (chapter 4).[48]

Chapter 3

Mental Causation: The Backlash and Free Lunches

The problem of mental causation is coeval with the mind-body problem—Descartes invented them both, or at least was responsible for them. For Descartes, mental causation became a problem—ultimately an insuperable one—because of his ontology of two radically diverse sorts of substances—material bodies whose essence is having a bulk in space and minds with consciousness as their essence. It is part of the common lore of western philosophy that Descartes invited the difficulty for himself by wanting too much—he wanted not only a sharply dualist ontology of mental and material substances but also an intimate causal commerce across the two domains. As we all know, many of Descartes's contemporaries immediately pounced on what they perceived to be a fatal flaw in the Cartesian position: How could such disparate substances, one extended in space and the other essentially lacking in spatial properties, causally influence one another, or "intermingle," as Descartes said, to form a "union" that we call a human being?

One of the surprising developments in the philosophy of mind during the past two decades or so has been the return of the mind-body problem—not as a problem for the substance dualists, a breed that has virtually vanished from the scene,[1] but as a threat to the physicalists who aspire to take mentality seriously. And there is an instructive parallel between Descartes's mind-body problem and the way the current debate on mind-body causation arose. For it was Davidson's anomalous monism that first touched off the current worries about mental causation, although, as we saw in yesterday's lecture, the problem has since taken many other shapes and directions. In a way that is reminiscent of Descartes's sharp separation of mind from matter, Davidson conceived of mental phenomena as constitutively distinct from physical phenomena. The mental, according to him, is essentially normative and regulated by the principles of rationality, whereas these normative constraints have no place in the physical domain. This constitutive difference between the mental and the physical is the essential premise from which Davidson argues for his "anomalism of the mental," the claim that there are no "strict" causal/predictive laws in the mental domain, and in particular no laws connecting mental phenomena with physical phenomena.[2] And yet, like Descartes, Davidson wanted causal interaction between mental and physical events as another fundamental component of his theory of the mind—it is one of the three basic "premises" from which he derives his anomalous monism. Again, in a way that is interestingly reminiscent of the reaction of Descartes's contemporaries to his interactionist dualism, critics and commentators of Davidson wasted no time in pouncing on his dualism of mental and physical properties, arguing in unison that anomalous monism renders mental properties of events causally irrelevant.[3] The only difference between Descartes and Davidson is that for the former it was the dualism of substances that caused the trouble, while for the latter it was his dualism of properties. For both the difficulty the critics saw arose from a serious, and well-founded, doubt that mind-body causation could be made consistent with the dualism each espoused.

The debate about mental causation that ensued from Davidson's anomalous monism has concerned the causal efficacy, or relevance, of mental properties vis-à-vis physical properties. This new problem was then seen to generalize beyond Davidson's anomalous monism, to apply to all forms of nonreductive physicalism, or property dualism, which has been the orthodoxy since the demise of the mind-brain identity theory, or, more broadly, reductive type physicalism. Again, the question at bottom has always been this: if mental properties are physically irreducible and remain outside the physical domain, then, given that the physical domain is causally closed, how can they exercise causal powers, or enjoy any kind of causal relevance, in the physical domain?

One sort of reaction on the part of some philosophers, which has gained significant popularity, to the reemergence of mental causation as a philosophical problem is to try to dissipate it by arguing that there is in fact no such "problem" worth worrying about, or, at any rate, to downplay its philosophical significance. It has been argued that worries about mental causation arise out of our misplaced philosophical priorities; that overindulgence in unmotivated metaphysical assumptions and arguments is the source of the unnecessary worries; that a misunderstanding of the logic and metaphysics of causation is at the core of the apparent troubles; that we should look to explanations and explanatory practices, not to metaphysics, for guidance on the matter of mental causation; that if there are problems about mental causation, exactly the same problems would arise for macrolevel causation in general, including causation in all the special sciences—for, say, biological causation and chemical causation; and so on.

Another related type of reaction has been to offer solutions at minimal philosophical costs—that is, to show that the problem can be solved in a simple and easy way, without having to pay a heavy metaphysical price, like giving up property dualism and embracing either reductionism or eliminativism, or trying to live with epiphenomenalism, or even seriously contemplating a return to substantival dualism. These are what we might call "free lunch" solutions—or, if not entirely free, at least pretty cheap ones.

My aim here is to examine some of these deflationary strategies for coping with the problem of mental causation. I will argue that none of them really succeed, and that we cannot make the problem go away by making simple and inexpensive repairs here and there. I believe that the problem goes deep, deep into our fundamental metaphysical views about ourselves and the world we live in, and that we need to make fairly drastic adjustments if we are serious about coming to terms with the problem. When we are properly done with the problem, our metaphysics of the mind would have undergone some serious alterations. There are no free lunches in philosophy any more than in real life, and I believe the cheap ones aren't worth the money. We might as well go for the real stuff and pay the price. When substance dualism was confronted by the problem of mental causation, dualism was the loser: mental substance is no longer with us. History may very well repeat itself: in the confrontation between property dualism and mental causation, dualism may again lose out, leaving irreducible mental properties in the dust.

Unavoidability of Metaphysics: The Exclusion Problem

Some philosophers have argued that if we would only free ourselves from our metaphysical preoccupations and attend to our actual explanatory practices involving mental phenomena, we would stop worrying about mental causation and learn to love it. Tyler Burge is an example; he writes:

> But what interests me more is the very existence of the worries. I think that they are symptomatic of a mistaken set of philosophical priorities. Materialist metaphysics has been given more weight than it deserves. Reflection on explanatory practice has been given too little. The metaphysical grounds that support the worries are vastly less strong than the more ordinary grounds we already have for rejecting them.[4]

What are the "ordinary grounds" that undermine the "metaphysical grounds" of materialism? Burge goes on:

> I think it more natural and fruitful to begin by assuming, defeasibly perhaps but firmly, that attributions of intentional mental events are central to psychological explanation both in ordinary life and in various parts of psychology. We may also assume that intentional mental events are often causes and that psychological explanation is often a form of causal explanation. Given these assumptions, the 'worry' about epiphenomenalism seems very re-

mote. . . . None of the metaphysical considerations advanced in current discussion seem to me remotely strong enough to threaten this conclusion.[5]

In a similar vein Lynne Rudder Baker has argued that all that we need to do to dissipate the problem of mind-body causation is to reverse our priorities between metaphysics and explanation. She urges:

My suggestion is to take as our philosophical starting point, not a metaphysical doctrine about the nature of causation or of reality, but a range of explanations that have been found worthy of acceptance. . . . If we reverse the priority of explanation and causation that is favoured by the metaphysician, the problem of mental causation just melts away. We begin with the question: Does what we think ever affect what we do? . . . With the reversal of priority of cause and explanation, the metaphysical version of the question does not arise, and the original question has an easy answer.[6]

Baker and Burge are clearly right on one point. As Burge says, our confidence in the truth of familiar intentional explanations does exceed our commitment to any recondite metaphysical principles. In this sense the epiphenomenalist "worries" are overstated. But I doubt that very many of us who have "worried" about mental causation have actually been concerned about the possibility that our thoughts and desires might turn out to have no powers to move our limbs. Our worries are not *evidential* or *epistemological* worries. Burge is right when he says that there is an air of make-believe about the epiphenomenalist threats, likening epiphenomenalism with epistemological skepticism. But what all this shows is that the problem of mental causation is primarily a metaphysical problem. It is the problem of showing *how* mental causation is possible, not *whether* it is possible, although of course what happens with the how-question may in the end induce us to reconsider our stance on the whether-question. In raising the how-question, we are assuming, "defeasibly but firmly" as Burge says, that the whether-question has already been affirmatively answered.[7] If, as Burge suggests, the problem of mental causation is on a par with the problem of epistemological skepticism, it should be problem enough. Just as reflections on skeptical arguments have deepened our understanding of the nature and limits of human knowledge, "worries" about epiphenomenalism may well lead to a deeper understanding of just what our mentality consists in and how it is related to our physical nature.

But metaphysical questions don't just pop up, out of nowhere. As I noted in yesterday's lecture, the how-question of mental causation arises because there are certain other commitments, whether metaphysical or of other sorts, that demand our presumptive respect but that make mental causation prima facie problematic. The issue is not metaphysics versus explanatory practice, as Burge would have it, nor metaphysics versus epistemology, as Baker would have it. Nor is the issue one of choosing between metaphysics and mental causation: most of us have already chosen mental causation, although as philosophers we should regard pretty much everything ultimately negotiable. The issue is *how to make our metaphysics consistent with mental causation,* and the choice that we need to make is between various *metaphysical alternatives,* not between some recondite metaphysical principle on the one hand and some cherished epistemological practice or principle on the other. This of course is not to say that metaphysics and epistemology are necessarily independent; as we will see below, epistemology and metaphysics do have something to do with each other in this area, and the choices we make in one can require adjustments and accommodations in the other.

Would the problem of mental causation take its leave if we did less metaphysics, as Burge and Baker urge, and instead focused our attention on psychological explanation? Burge says that "our understanding of mental causation derives primarily from our understanding of mentalistic explanation."[8] But what is our understanding of mentalistic explanation? Burge doesn't address this question directly, but we can see what he has in mind: mentalistic explanations—explanations that invoke mental states in their explanantia—are often causal explanations. In the second quoted passage above he says that "we may assume that intentional mental states are often causes and that psychological explanation is often a form of causal explanation." As some of you may recall, there was a prolonged debate in the 1950s and 1960s, no less intense than the current debate on mental causation, on the question whether belief-desire explanations of action are causal explanations or whether "reasons are causes." Largely due to the confluence of various philosophical influences including Wittgenstein and the British school of ordinary language philosophy, the anticausal position had very much the upper hand for many years,[9] until Davidson's causal theory overturned it and became the new orthodoxy in the late 1960s and early 1970s.[10] If, as Burge says, we "may assume" that belief-desire explanation is a form of causal explanation, we owe this license substantially to Davidson. What carried the day for the causal view was Davidson's philosophical argument, not the pervasiveness of our explanatory practice of rationalizing actions in terms of belief and desire. There was no disagreement on the explanatory practice; the debate was about its nature and rationale.

Moreover Davidson's own account of rationalizing explanation as causal explanation involved not an insubstantial amount of metaphysics—to mention a couple of its key components, a view about singular causal statements and their relationship to general causal laws and a much-debated theory about events and their descriptions. A full statement of his argument is likely to implicate the whole metaphysical package of anomalous monism, including the controversial doctrine of the anomalism of the mental. Much of the current debate on mental causation has stemmed from a widely shared dissatisfaction with Davidson's account—the worry that Davidson's theory does not accord mental kinds and properties an appropriate causal role in behavior production.[11] Surely this brief history should suffice to persuade us that we cannot easily insulate the explanatory practice of behavior rationalization from metaphysical involvements. The question whether rationalizations are a species of causal explanation itself involves substantive metaphysical issues.

Even after we have answered this question—affirmatively, let us assume—metaphysics still won't go away. For the only way in which I believe that we can understand the idea of causal explanation presupposes the idea that the event invoked in a causal explanation is in reality a cause of the phenomenon to be explained. That is, if c (or a description or representation of c) causally explains e, c must *be* a cause of e. If my desire for a drink of water causally explains my body's movement toward the kitchen, the desire must really be a cause of the bodily movement. I take this to be an untendentious and uncontroversial point.

Suppose then that my desire for water causes a certain motion of my body. This is a case of mental-to-physical causation. So far so good. But metaphysical problems begin to emerge in several ways. First, suppose that we trace the causal chain back from my bodily motion—to simplify, the movement of my left foot as I take my first step toward the kitchen. I assume we have a pretty good neurophysiological story to tell about how such limb motion occurs, a story involving transmission of neural signals, contraction of a group of muscles, and so on; let us suppose that the story ends with some neural event in my central nervous system, presumably the firing of a group of neural fibers somewhere deep in the brain. There seems every reason to think that such a neurophysiological causal explanation also exists; at least, we cannot rule out such a possibility. What then is the relationship between this explanation and the intentional explanation in terms of my belief and desire? One invokes a neural state, N, as a cause of my foot movement; the other invokes my desire for a drink of water, as a cause of the very same event. How are these two causes related to each other?

When we are faced with two purported causes, or causal explanations, of a single event, the following alternative accounts of the situation are initially available: (a) each is a sufficient cause and the effect is causally overdetermined, (b) they are each necessary and jointly help make up a sufficient cause (that is, each is only a "partial cause"), (c) one is part of the other, (d) the causes are in fact one and the same but given under different descriptions, (e) one (presumably the mental cause in the present case) is in some appropriate sense reducible to the other, and (f) one (again the mental cause) is a derivative cause with its causal status dependent in some sense on the neural cause, N. Perhaps there are others, but it is clear that for our present case, most of them, including (a), (b), and (c), are nonstarters. The general point I want to stress is this: the presence of two causal stories, each claiming to offer a full causal account of a given event, creates an unstable situation requiring us to find an account of how the two purported causes are related to each other. This is the problem of "causal/explanatory exclusion."[12]

Burge, as I take it, would reply that intentional explanations and physiological explanations need not, and do not, compete with each other. He says:

> It would be perverse to think that the mentalistic explanation excludes or interferes with non-intentional explanation of the physical movement. I think that these ideas seem perverse not because we know that the mental events are material. They seem perverse because we know that the two causal explanations are explaining the same physical effect as the outcome of two very different patterns of events. The explanations of these patterns answer two very different types of inquiry. Neither type of explanation makes essential, specific assumptions about the other. . . . The perversity of thinking that mental causes must fill gaps in physical chains of events probably has its source in traditional dualism, or in libertarian worries about free will.[13]

No, "the perversity" has nothing to do with dualism or free will; it has only to do with two causal claims, each purporting to provide a sufficient cause of a single effect. The interesting fact about explanations that Burge misses is that *two or more explanations can be rival explanations even though their explanatory premises are mutually consistent and in fact all true, if they purport to explain (in particular, causally explain) a single explanandum.* That the explanations arise in different areas of inquiry, that they are given at "different levels" of analysis or description, or that they are responses to different epistemic or pragmatic concerns, makes no difference. Thus a car accident is explained by a highway designer as having been caused by the incorrect camber of the highway curve, and by a police officer as caused by the inattentive driving of an inexperienced driver. But in a case like this we naturally think of the offered causes as partial causes; they together help make up a full and sufficient cause of the accident. As long as each claims to be a full cause of the event to be explained, a tension is created and we are entitled to ask, indeed compelled to ask, how the two purported causes are related to each other. In fact, it is precisely because "neither . . . explanation makes essential, specific assumptions about the other" that we need to know how the two explanations are related, how the two causal stories about a single phenomenon mesh with each other. Are the two stories at bottom one story couched in different languages? Do the two stories supplement one another, each being only partial? And so on. Metaphysics is the domain where different languages, theories, explanations, and conceptual systems come together and have their mutual ontological relationships sorted out and clarified. That there is such a common domain is the assumption of a broad and untendentious realism about our cognitive activities. If you believe that there is no such common domain, well, that's metaphysics, too.

The problem of causal/explanatory exclusion arises if there are cases of psychological explanations of physical behavior in which we are prepared to believe that the physical effect has, or must have, a physical causal explanation as well. And we do not need to subscribe to a general doctrine of the causal closure of the physical domain to believe that there indeed must be such cases; the physical causal closure only makes the exclusion problem a general one for all mentalistic explanations of physical behavior. To appreciate the exclusion problem, we do not require much heavy-duty metaphysics—overarching doctrines about mental anomalism, "strict laws" in causal relations, a physical/mechanical conception of causality, token physicalism, and the rest. It arises from the very notion of causal explanation and what strikes me as a perfectly intuitive and ordinary understanding of the causal relation. If this is right, turning away from metaphysics to embrace epistemology, or away from causation to embrace explanation, will not dissipate the need for an account of mental causation. There is a short and straight route from mentalistic explanation to mental causation, and from the possibility of dual explanations of a physical occurrence to the vexing problem of causal/explanatory causation.

It is interesting to note that both Burge and Baker, in their papers, explicitly acknowledge some form of mind-body supervenience or dependence. Burge writes:

> There are surely some systematic, even necessary, relations between mental events and underlying physical processes. We have good be reason to believe that mental processes depend on underlying physical processes.[14]

Although Burge isn't very specific on the nature of the dependence he posits between the mental and the physical, we may safely assume that it must at least come to supervenience. In contrast, Baker explicitly acknowledges the mind-body dependence in the sense of strong supervenience (see chapter 1). She thinks that the doctrine she calls "SS" (for strong mind-body supervenience) is an "idle speculation," but she is willing to let it be and focus her attack on causation. In any case, if Baker and Burge accept mind-body supervenience, they need to respond to the supervenience argument of my last lecture: they need to tell us how they would resist the chain of reasoning that apparently leads from mind-body supervenience to an epiphenomenalist conclusion.

Do Counterfactuals Help?

In a recent paper Terence Horgan, whose work in this area has been important and influential, addresses the issue of mental causation and reductionism, writing:

Regarding causal-exclusion reasoning, I advocate robust causal compatibilism—as indeed I think any philosopher must do who espouses nonreductive materialism. I certainly acknowledge that my compatibilism needs articulation and defense; that is an important philosophical project . . .

First, how might the view be articulated and defended? Robust causal compatibilism is a byproduct of a general conception of causal properties and of causal explanation that I think is credible and well motivated apart from worries about causal exclusion. The leading idea is that causal properties are ones that figure in robust, objective, patterns of diachronic counterfactual dependence among properties . . .

Higher-order causal natural-kind properties, according to such views, are ones that figure centrally in the relevant higher-order dependence-patterns and nomic generalizations. As such, these properties need not be nomically coextensive with lower-order causal properties—not even locally coextensive by conforming to species-relative or structure-relative biconditional bridge laws. Instead, higher-order causal properties can perfectly well crossclassify lower-order ones, even locally for a given species of creatures and for single individuals within a species.[15]

As I take it, Horgan's suggestion that higher-order properties "cross-classify" lower-order ones is meant to suggest the causal/theoretical autonomy of the special sciences in relation to physical theory. Since this is a point often made by nonreductive physicalists as an argument for the irreducibility of higher-order properties, let us briefly look at what is involved. To begin, what does "cross-classify" mean in this context? To say a given taxonomic system cross-classifies another must mean something like this: there are items that are classified in the same way, and cannot be distinguished, by the second taxonomy (that is, indiscernible in respect of properties recognized in this taxonomy) but that are classified differently according to the first taxonomy (that is, discernible in respect of properties recognized in that taxonomy), and perhaps vice versa. That is, a taxonomy cross-classifies another just in case the former makes distinctions that cannot be made by the latter (and perhaps also conversely). But then this means that the first taxonomy fails to supervene on the second, and Horgan's claim when understood this way must come to the denial of supervenience of higher-order properties. If mental properties and biological properties cross-classify basic physical properties, they cannot supervene on the latter. This is an interesting suggestion. The claim is that certain higher-order properties of physical systems are not supervenient on their physical properties, and that they are nomically connected to each other by higher-order laws irreducible to more basic laws. These higher-order laws would generate an autonomous causal domain that need not answer to the more basic physical causal domain. This is a serious form of dualism, perhaps an approach worthy of serious consideration. In denying supervenience, however, it falls short of minimal physicalism, and for this reason I am uncertain whether this is what Horgan really intends. I think that in talking about cross-classifying, he may simply be referring to the familiar claim of multiple realizability of higher-order properties in relation to basic physical properties. As we saw in the first lecture, the idea that mental properties are physically realized, whether multiply or uniquely, logically entails the supervenience thesis. If you accept physical realizationism, as I believe Horgan does, you cannot at the same time hold the "cross-classification" thesis, at least in the present sense.

Let us return to the other theme in Horgan, namely that the causal exclusion problem can be avoided if we choose to base our causal claims on counterfactual dependencies. This is a popular approach, advocated by a number of philosophers. Lynne Baker is one of them; she says that an "easy" answer to the question "Does what we think ever affect what we do?" is forthcoming when we reflect on certain counterfactuals. For example, to see that Jill's thought that she left her keys on the counter and her wanting them back caused her to return to the bookstore, all we need to do, Baker says, is to appreciate the following "explanatory fact": "If she hadn't thought that she had left her keys, then, other things being equal, she wouldn't have returned to the bookstore; and given that she did think that she had left her keys, then, other things being equal, her returning was inevitable."[16] Tyler Burge appears to have something similar in mind when he says: " . . . one can specify various ways in which mental causes 'make a difference' which do not conflict with physical explanations. The differences they make are specified by psychological causal explanations, and by counterfactuals associated with these explanations."[17]

Let us briefly look at Baker's suggestion. Her idea is to explain causation in terms of explanation (so that "causation becomes an explanatory concept"[18]) and then explain explanation in terms of appropriate counterfactuals and the "inevitability" of the outcome given the putative cause. We can agree with Baker, Horgan, Burge, and others that our confidence in the reality of mental causation is grounded, substantially if not wholly, in our acceptance of such explanations and counterfactuals. (Not wholly because surely our belief in mental causation is inseparable from our view of ourselves as agents—that is, the belief that our desires, beliefs, and intentions can, and do, cause us to move our limbs in appropriate ways and thereby rearrange things around us.) We can also agree that our explanatory practices involving intentional states and actions must be respected in any discussion of mental causation. However, an appeal to familiar counterfactuals involving mental states will not make the need of further metaphysical clarification go away. We can see this, I think, in connection with Baker's proposal. For consider the epiphenomenalist who claims that some neural state, N, was the cause of both Jill's thought that she left her keys at the bookstore counter and of her returning to the bookstore. The epiphenomenalist may well be prepared to accept both clauses of Baker's explanatory/counterfactual gloss on the causal claim, for he might reason as follows: "If Jill's thought had not occurred, then Jill would not have been in N, and given that Jill's thought did occur, N must have occurred, and this made Jill's return inevita-

ble." It seems to me that there is no incoherence in this epiphenomenalist account of the situation. I am not saying that an
epiphenomenalist account of this form will work in every case;
the point is only that it is not ruled out by Baker's proposals.

In more general terms, the counterfactual test is a poor test to
assess causal directionality: given that c caused e, the "backtrack-
ing" counterfactual "if e had not occurred, c would not have
occurred either" can often be defended, on almost any model of
counterfactuals.[19] Also, when e_1 and e_2 are collateral effects of a
single common cause c, the counterfactual "If e_1 had not occurred, e_2 would not have" and its converse can both be true, and
there are likely to be cases of this kind where it is true to say that
"given e_1, e_2 was inevitable." Moreover the concept of "inevitability" invoked by Baker seems badly in need of further clarification; saying "given c, e is inevitable" sounds very much like just
another way of saying "c (causally) necessitates e"—a concept
that has been the nemesis of the Humeans. Unless Baker can
provide us with a nonquestion-begging explanation of the notion of inevitability involved, her project of replacing causation
with explanation must be judged incomplete. The problem of
mental causation won't just "melt away."

To summarize our discussion of the counterfactual approach
then, what the counterfactual theorists need to do is to give an
account of just what makes those mind-body counterfactuals we
want for mental causation true, and show that on that account
those counterfactuals we don't want, for example, epiphenomenalist counterfactuals, turn out to be false. Merely to point to
the apparent truth, and acceptability, of certain mind-body counterfactuals as a vindication of mind-body causation is to mis-
construe the philosophical task at hand. It has no greater
philosophical significance as regards the problem of mental causation than pointing to the truth of sundry "because" statements
involving mental states. Such gestures only show that mind-
body causation is part of what we normally take to be the real
world; they go no further than a mere reaffirmation of our belief
in the reality of mental causation. What we want—at least, what
some of us are looking for—is a philosophical account of *how* it

can be real in light of other principles and truths that seem to be forced upon us.[20]

"Program Explanation" and Supervenient Causation

Frank Jackson and Philip Pettit have recently proposed what they call "program explanation" to account for the causal/ explanatory relevance of the mental.[21] In stressing explanation their approach resembles that of Baker and others. However, in a crucial respect it is different, since Jackson and Pettit begin by accepting the premise that the mental lacks causal *efficacy:* it is causal *relevance* that they hope to save for the mental through its role in "program explanations." Consider an example: we explain the breaking of a vase by pointing to its fragility. But a set of intuitively plausible principles, Jackson and Pettit argue, leads to the conclusion that the causally efficacious property in this situation is the molecular structure of the glass of which the vase is made, not the vase's fragility. Again, this problem appears to be what we have called "the exclusion problem." We will not go into the principles that, according to Jackson and Pettit, lead to this conclusion, nor their definition of causal efficacy; instead, we will focus on their strategy for saving an explanatory/causal role for fragility, its assumed lack of causal efficacy notwithstanding. For if their strategy has merit, it could be one way in which mental causation can be saved—especially, since their problem, like ours, appears to be that of causal exclusion.

The main idea that drives Jackson and Pettit's approach is that a property, F, which is causally *inefficacious* in bringing about an instantiation of another property G, can yet be *relevant* in the causation of an instance of G in virtue of the fact that "G occurred because F occurred" is a good "program explanation." But what is a program explanation? According to Jackson and Pettit, "G occurred because F occurred" can be a good, informative explanation in one of two ways: (i) F is a causally efficacious property with respect to G, or (ii) F "programs for," or "ensures," the presence of some property, P, which is causally efficacious with respect to *G*, although *F* itself lacks causal efficacy in relation to *G*. (This evidently allows for different causally efficacious properties, *Ps*, for different instances of *F*.) We can see how this works in the case of the fragile vase and its breaking: although fragility is not itself causally efficacious, and fails to be a productive cause of the breaking, it is nonetheless causally relevant in that it programs for, or ensures, the presence of a causally efficacious property, that is, the specific molecular structure of the glass. As they put it, "although not efficacious itself, [fragility] was such that its realization ensured that there was an efficacious property in the offing."[22] Where does the term "program" come from? Jackson and Pettit write:

> The property-instance does not figure in the productive process leading to the event but it more or less ensures that a property-instance which is required for that process does figure. A useful metaphor for describing the role of the property is to say that its realization programs for the appearance of the productive property and, under a certain description, for the event produced. The analogy is with a computer program which ensures that certain things will happen—things satisfying certain descriptions—though all the work of producing those things goes on at a lower, mechanical level.[23]

A computational explanation that purports to explain a given step in a computational process in terms of earlier computational stages therefore is a program explanation; the earlier stages are causally inefficacious, though explanatorily relevant, for the explanandum, with all the genuine causal processes taking place at the electronic level. Jackson and Pettit believe that this approach will save explanations in the special sciences, including psychology:

> . . . though we shall not explore the cases here, it seems to extend to explanations in common sense and the special sciences: for example, to explanations in sociology which invoke a property like group-cohesion, to explanations in

psychology which invoke attitudinal contents as causally relevant properties, and to explanations in biology which appeal to a property such as that of maximizing inclusive fitness. In all such cases it is hard to see how the explanations can have the interest they clearly possess other than through being the programming variety.[24]

What should we think of this proposal? Let us first note that this approach does not substantially differ from what I used to advocate as a way of handling mental causation—the model of "supervenient causation." Here the main idea is that a property can derive its causal role, and have a role in causal explanation, in virtue of its supervenience on a property involved in causal processes. Suppose that F has $P_1, \ldots, P_n$ as its supervenience bases. This means that whenever F is instantiated, one of its base properties, P_i, is instantiated. Suppose further that each of these Ps is causally productive of an effect G. We can then say that F is a "supervenient cause" of G. That was the idea of supervenient causation. But it is clear that this nicely fits the model of program explanation. The occurrence of F "ensures" or "programs for" an occurrence of one of these causally efficacious base properties, Ps. The two models appear to come to pretty much the same thing; at least, where there is supervenient causation in the above sense there will be a program explanation and causal relevance in Jackson and Pettit's sense.

Since Jackson and Pettit begin with the assumption that mental properties, and properties of the special sciences, lack causal efficacy, it seems fair enough to consider them epiphenomenalists. And it is worth noting that the model of program explanation is something that is entirely consistent with epiphenomenalism. Like the supervenience theorist, the epiphenomenalist can perfectly well say that the occurrence of, say, a pain, "ensures" or "programs for" the presence of its neural cause, say the firings of C-fibers, and it is this neural event that caused me to wince. As we have already noted, epiphenomenalism is committed to mind-body supervenience.

Since Jackson and Pettit concede the causal impotence of the mental, the vindication of mental causation cannot be something they seek. Given this, how appropriate is it to speak of the "causal relevance" of the mental? In the total absence of causal efficacy it is difficult to see how there can be room for causal relevance. The only relevance that is present here seems *informational* relevance: the occurrence of a programming property gives us information that some causally efficacious property is present and doing its work, though we may know not what. It would have been better for them to focus exclusively on the vindication of special-science explanations—that is, on vindicating the explanatory efficacy or relevance of special-science properties rather than their causal efficacy or relevance. The question then is this: Does the model of program explanation succeed in vindicating special-science explanations and in demonstrating the explanatory efficacy of special-science properties?

The answer evidently depends on your view of explanation. However, it is clear that program explanations, whatever their explanatory value, cannot be *causal* explanations (Jackson and Pettit don't claim that they are), and the "because" in "Doreen winced because she felt a sharp pain in her elbow" cannot be read as invoking a causal relation between Doreen's pain and her wincing any more than the "because" in "The vase broke because it was fragile" can be given such a reading. To repeat a point I have made before, a causal explanation of an event that invokes another as its cause can be a correct explanation only if the putative cause really is a cause of the event to be explained. Any weaker conception would merely cheapen the idea of causal explanation.

But if you are willing to give up on mental causation and a robust notion of mental causal explanation, and live with a looser and weaker model of explanatory relevance, you can perhaps make use of David Lewis's idea that "to explain an event is to provide some information about its causal history,"[25] with a simple but not insubstantial alteration. An alteration is required because on Lewis's notion the causal history of an event includes itself, any of its parts, and is closed under causal dependence. That is, any event on which an event in a causal history is dependent is part of the same history. However, causal histories are not closed under the converse of causal dependence, and in consequence epiphenomena of an event are not part of its causal history. This means that, on Lewis's model, the invoking of an epiphenomenon (say, pain) of the real cause (neuronal firings) of the event to be explained will not count as an explanation, or causal explanation, of that event. What can be done is to define, say, the "causal network" of an event, which is closed under both causal dependence and its converse,[26] and then explain the idea of explanation in terms of providing information about the causal network in which an event is embedded. Pointing to an epiphenomenon of a true cause of an event does give some causal information about the event.

I believe it is only this sort of extremely relaxed, loose notion of explanation that can accommodate Jackson and Pettit's program explanations. Explanation is a pretty loose and elastic notion—essentially as loose and elastic as the underlying notions of understanding and making something intelligible—and no one should legislate what counts and what doesn't count as explanation, excepting only this, namely that when we speak of "causal explanation," we should insist, as I said, that what is invoked as a cause really be a cause of whatever it is that is being explained. Realism about explanation should at least cover causal explanation. The main question about program explanation then is this: Is a notion of explanation this loose and relaxed any way of vindicating explanations invoking special-science properties, in particular, psychological properties?

Here I expect people to disagree, and that, I believe, only reflects the elasticity of the notion of explanation. But I am inclined to believe that this way of saving the explanatory relevance or efficacy, or whatever else you may choose to call it, is too weak to be satisfying. To my mind any vindication of psychological explanation worth having must do justice to the "because" in "She winced because she felt a sudden sharp pain in the elbow," and to do this we need a more robust sense of "because" than is provided by program explanation.

Does the Problem of Mental Causation Generalize?

Jackson and Pettit, as well as Horgan, treat mental causation only as a special case of the problem of causation in the special sciences—causation involving "higher-order" properties and events. Commendably these writers take the general problem seriously and offer ways of solving, or dissolving, the problem. In contrast, there are those who appear to believe that the supposed generalizability of the problem of mental causation to other areas, as biology and geology, only goes to show that the problem is a bogus problem, something not worth worrying about. In the following passage Burge expresses just such an attitude:

> The existence of a closed system reflects a pattern of causal relations and of causal explanation that needs no supplementation from the outside. There are no gaps. It does not follow from this that such a system excludes or overrides causal relations or causal explanation in terms of properties from outside the system. Indeed, if it did follow, as often been pointed out, there would be no room for causal efficacy in the special sciences, even in natural sciences like chemistry and physiology. For there is no gap (other than perhaps quantum gaps) in the causal relations explained in terms of the properties of physics. But few are tempted by the idea that physical events cannot be caused in virtue of physiological properties of physical events.[27]

Burge's claim is that if the causal closure of the physical domain excluded mental-to-physical causation (that is, the causal efficacy of mental properties in relation to physical properties), the same considerations would show that no special-science properties could be causally efficacious with respect to their underlying lower-level properties. To put it another way, just as the causal closure of the fundamental physical domain does not exclude the causal efficacy of properties in the physical special sciences, like chemistry and biology, the causal closure of the physical domain (taken as a whole, to include biology, chemistry, etc.) does not exclude the causal efficacy of mental properties.

Reasoning of this sort seems widespread. Baker too writes:

> Moreover, I want to show that the metaphysical assumptions with which we began inevitably lead to scepticism not only about the efficacy of contentful thought, but about macro-causation generally. But if we lack warrant for claiming that macro-properties are generally causally relevant, and if we take explanations to mention causes, then most, if not all, of the putative explanations that are routinely offered and accepted in science and everyday life are not explanatory at all.[28]

Note that Baker mentions all *macrolevel causation* as being jeopardized by "the metaphysical assumptions" (which, by the way, include mind-body supervenience), all causation being monopolized by microphysical processes. Robert Van Gulick, too, brings up the threat of microphysical causal monopoly:

> . . . reserving causal status for strictly physical properties . . . would make not only intentional properties epiphenomenal, it would also make the properties of chemistry, biology, neurophysiology and every theory outside microphysics epiphenomenal . . . If the only sense in which intentional properties are epiphenomenal is a sense in which chemical and geological properties are also epiphenomenal, need we have any real concern about their status: they seem to be in the best of company and no one seems worried about the causal status of chemical properties.[29]

(This is a little like being told that we shouldn't worry about, say, being depressed because everyone else has the same problem.) Perhaps no one is worried about the causal efficacy of chemical properties or biological properties, but then not many people are really worried about mental causation either. What some of us are worried about is finding an intelligible *account* of mental causation. This is a different worry and, I dare say, a philosophically legitimate one. Do we have an account of causal efficacy for chemical or biological properties in relation to fundamental physical properties? Perhaps everyone believes that we can find one without too much trouble. But I certainly cannot think one up on demand, and if anyone else can, I would like to see it put down on paper. (If anyone is inclined to retort, "Who *needs* an account of how chemical or biological properties have causal efficacy?" I hope you will agree that that is not a philosophical attitude we should recommend.) Further, how can we be sure that an account that works, say, for chemical properties will work as well in the mental-physical case?

What forms the background of the issues being raised here is the standard hierarchical picture of the world that I discussed in the first lecture. Things of this world, and of their properties, are pictured in a vertically organized hierarchical system, micro to macro, from the elementary particles of microphysics to atoms and molecules, and their aggregates, and then upward to cells and organisms, and so on—a picture that is implicit in the familiar talk of levels and orders—as in "level of organization," "level of description," "level of analysis," "level of explanation," and the like. As you will recall, Horgan, Jackson, and Pettit, and others cast their arguments in terms of "higher-order" properties of the special sciences; if there is "higher-order," there must also be "lower-order," and this again suggests an ordered hierarchy of properties.

It is clear that our thinking about mentality and psychology has been shaped by this picture: psychology is a special science located at one of these levels, toward the higher end, in this multilayered system, and mentality is a distinctive set of properties that make their first appearance at this level. It is natural for those who share this picture to see nothing special about mental causation: if there is a difficulty at the mental level vis-à-vis the lower neural/biological level, we should expect the same difficulty to attend every level in relation to its lower levels.

Since there is, or at least appears to be, no special problem at these lower levels, why should we think there is a problem at the mental level? The implied answer is no. Let us call this "the generalization argument."

In my second lecture we saw how a problem about mental causation can be seen to arise from the doctrine of mind-body supervenience. Our discussion there did not require an elaborate characterization of the supervenience relation involved, or any special characteristic of the mental except for its supervenience. Reasoning that leads to the generalization argument is based on the assumption that the mental-neural relationship is, in all relevant respects, the same relationship that characterizes, say, the chemical-microphysical, biological-physicochemical, or other interlevel cases. The supervenience argument, if correct, shows that where there is supervenience there is a potential problem about the causal efficacy of the supervenient properties in relation to their base properties. It would seem then that the generalization argument applies directly to the supervenience argument, and this may give us a possible strategy for dealing with it. We will consider the issues raised by the generalization argument in the balance of this lecture, returning to them briefly again in my final lecture.

Properties: "Levels" and "Orders"

Let us return to the idea that mental properties are "realized" by physical/neural properties, or what is usually taken to be an equivalent idea that mental properties are the "roles" of which the physical/neural properties are the "occupants." It is often assumed that this realization relation is what generates the hierarchical ordering of levels. William Lycan is very explicit about this:

> Very generally put, my [point] is that 'software'/'hardware' talk encourages the idea of a bipartite Nature, divided into two levels, roughly the physicochemical and the (supervenient) 'functional' or higher-organizational—as against real-

ity, which is multiple *hierarchy* of levels of nature, each level marked by nexus of nomic generalizations and supervenient on all those levels below it on the continuum. See Nature as hierarchically organized in this way, and the 'function'/'structure' distinction *goes relative:* something is a role as opposed to occupant, a functional state as opposed to a realizer, or vice versa, only *modulo* a designated level of nature.[30]

We have already discussed Block's epiphenomenalist worries concerning the causal status of functionally defined second-order properties—whether dormitivity, as a second-order property distinct from its first-order chemical realizers, can be accorded causal powers to put people to sleep.[31] But does Block's problem generalize? It's clear from the example of dormitivity, the same problem can arise in different areas—different levels, if you wish. Think of importing Block's problem into the hierarchy of the sort pictured by Lycan: neural realizers of pain are themselves second-order with respect to certain lower-level properties (which preempt their causal powers), the latter in turn are second-order to their lower-level properties, and so on ad infinitum, until you reach the rock bottom level of microphysics (if such a level exists), which turns out to be the only level where genuine causal powers reside. Whence Burge's, Baker's, and Van Gulick's claim that the usual worries about mental property epiphenomenalism lead to the consequence that all causal powers seep down and get deposited at the microphysical level, leaving microphysics as the only theory capable of generating causal explanations. As Baker worries, it would follow that all macrolevel causation is a mere illusion. The errant baseball didn't after all break the window, and the earthquake didn't cause the buildings to collapse! This strikes us as intolerable. What's more: What if there is no bottom level (as Block challenges us to consider[32])? It looks as though if there is no bottom level in this picture, causal powers would drain away into a bottomless pit and there wouldn't be any causation *anywhere!*

Lycan in the above quotation appears to think that his hierarchy of levels is generated by the operation of forming second-order functional properties, or, to look at the hierarchy in the other direction, by the realization relation, the relation that a first-order property bears to a second-order property whose functional specification ("role") it satisfies. We can clearly think of a hierarchy of properties generated this way. But notice the following important fact about this hierarchy: *this hierarchy does not parallel the micro-macro hierarchy*—to put it another way, *the realization relation does not track the micro-macro relation.* The reason is simple: *both second-order properties and their first-order realizers are properties of the same entities and systems.* The pill you ingest has both dormitivity and the chemical property which realizes dormitivity; you are in pain and have your c-fibers firing. It is evident that *a second-order property and its realizers are at the same level in the micro-macro hierarchy; they are properties of the very same objects.* This is a simple and direct consequence of the very concepts of "second-order property" and "realizer": for *something* to have a second-order property is for *it* to have one or another of its realizers, that is, a first-order property satisfying the specification that defines the second-order property. Consequently, when we talk of second-order properties and their realizers, there is no movement downward, or upward, in the hierarchy of entities and their properties ordered by the micro-macro relation. The series created by the second-order/realizer relation does not track the ordered series of micro-macro levels; it stays entirely within a single level in the micro-macro hierarchy.

An illusion of micro-macro movement is created, I believe, by the fact that in many philosophically interesting cases involving second-order properties, the first-order realizers are what we may call *micro-based (or microstructural) properties*, properties of a whole that are characterized in terms of its microstructure (we will shortly give a more precise explanation of this idea). But such properties are *macroproperties* (or, more precisely, properties at the same level as those they realize). It is clear that realizers of a second-order property are not always micro-based in this sense: having a primary color, as we saw, is a second-order property over the domain of colors, but its realizers are just colors. Whether or not colors are micro-based properties obviously is not an issue here. The question whether something is a realizer of a certain second-order property is independent of issues concerning any micro-macro considerations. The situation is the same with functional properties defined in terms of causal roles. Consider the functional second-order property: having a property that is caused to instantiate by tissue damage and whose instantiations cause wincings and cryings. There could be a Cartesian functionalist who takes phenomenal pain, not any neural state, as a realizer of this property. And it is clear that such a nonphysical functionalist can allow multiple Cartesian realizers for functionally defined psychological properties (of course such a person would not consider them "psychological" properties); she might allow that in some species the sensation of itch, or tickle, could realize functional pain.

I think we might usefully distinguish between "higher-level" and "higher-order," or "levels" and "orders," when speaking of properties in an ordering, using the "order" idiom for first-order, second-order, third-order, . . . , properties, and reserving the "level" idiom for tracking the micro-macro hierarchy. That itself is merely a terminological proposal, but there is an important distinction to appreciate. As we saw, the first-order/second-order/third-order . . . progression does not track the micro-macro ordering: these properties are all properties applying to entities at a single micro-macro level. In contrast, spin, charm, and such are properties of elementary particles, and they have no application to atoms, molecules, and higher objects in the micro-macro hierarchy; transparency and inflammability are properties of aggregates of molecules, and they have no place for atoms or more basic particles. Consciousness and intentionality are properties of biological organisms, or at least their neural systems, and they have no application to entities that are micro in relation to them. Having a mass of ten kilograms is a property of certain aggregates of molecules, like my coffee table. And it is a micro-based property of the table in the following sense: for my table to have this property is for it to consist of two parts, its top and its pedestal, such that the first has a mass of six kilograms and the second a mass of four kilograms.

I believe we can make use of David Armstrong's notion of "structural property"[33] to explain the idea of "micro-based property." We may say that:

> P is a *micro-based property* just in case P is the property of being completely decomposable into nonoverlapping proper parts, $a_1, a_2, \ldots, a_n$, such that $P_1(a_1), P_2(a_2), \ldots, P_n(a_n)$, and $R(a_1, \ldots, a_n)$.[34]

Being a water molecule therefore is a micro-based property in this sense: it is the property of having two hydrogen atoms and one oxygen atom in a such-and-such bonding relationship. A micro-based property therefore is constituted by micro-constituents—that is, by the micro-parts of the object that has it and the properties and relations characterizing these parts. But we should be clear that such properties are macroproperties, not microproperties.

These considerations suffice to show that the generalization argument does not have the full generality its supporters attribute to it. In particular, the exclusion-based worries about mental causation do not generalize across micro-macro levels. Consider Block's worries about second-order properties: here the main worry is that the causal role of a second-order property is threatened with preemption by its first-order realizers. As we noted, second-order properties and their realizers are all at the same level in the micro-macro hierarchy, and the causal worries about second-order properties are *intralevel* worries and do not cut across micro-macro boundaries. The exclusion-based arguments of the sort we considered in my second lecture therefore do not generalize across micro-macro levels, and do not have the dire consequence Block, Van Gulick, and others impute to them, namely that all causal powers might seep down, ending up deposited at the most basic level of microphysics, or draining away altogether if there is no such level.

That that cannot be so should be obvious from the most mundane examples. This table has a mass of ten kilograms, and this property, that of having a mass of ten kilograms, represents a well-defined set of causal powers. But no micro-constituent of this table, none of its proper parts, has this property or the causal powers it represents. H_2O molecules have causal powers that no oxygen or hydrogen atoms have. A neural assembly consisting of many thousands of neurons will have properties whose causal powers go beyond the causal powers of the properties of its constituent neurons, or subassemblies, and human beings have causal powers that none of our individual organs have. Clearly then *macroproperties can, and in general do, have their own causal powers, powers that go beyond the causal powers of their microconstituents.* This is an obvious but important point to keep in mind.

But what of the supervenience-inspired considerations against mental causation, of the sort we considered in my second lecture? Don't all properties supervene, as we saw in my first lecture, on lower-level properties in the micro-macro hierarchy, and ultimately on microphysical properties? And doesn't the argument of the second lecture ("the supervenience argument") show that the causal powers of the supervenient properties are threatened with preemption by their microphysical base properties?

The answer is that when we speak of microphysical or mereological supervenience—that is, the supervenience of all properties on microphysical properties and relations—we are speaking often quite loosely. We must see just what is involved in such a claim. Suppose that we say that a certain property P of something s supervenes on microphysical properties or facts about s. What we mean to say is that the fact that s has P, or whether or not s has P, is fixed once the micro-constituents of s and the properties and relations characterizing these constituents are fixed. This means that the base property on which P supervenes is a micro-based property, the property of having such-and-such proper parts that have such-and-such properties and are configured by such-and-such relations. This is a micro-based macroproperty of s, not a property that belongs to any of its proper parts. In general, supervenient properties and their base properties are instantiated by the same objects and hence are on the same level. This again is a simple consequence of the concept of supervenience: Socrates's goodness supervenes on his honesty, generosity, courage, and wisdom, and it is the same person, Socrates, who instantiates both these subvenient virtues and the supervenient goodness.

So microphysical, or mereological, supervenience does not track the micro-macro hierarchy any more than the realization relation does; the series of supervenient properties, one mereologically supervenient on the next, when we go deeper and deeper into the micro, remains at the same level in the micro-macro hierarchy, just as the properties ordered by the realization relation stay at the same level. This means that the supervenience argument, which exploits the supervenience relation, does not have the effect of emptying macrolevels of causal powers and rendering familiar macro-objects and their properties causally impotent.

This answers some, but not all, of the points raised by the generalization argument. The part that has been answered is the worry that the only causally active agents in this world might turn out to be basic particles and their microphysical properties, and that the familiar objects of our daily experience, like tables, chairs, and brains, and their properties might be deprived of causal powers. But there is a part of the generalization argument that has not been properly addressed, and it is this: If supervenience puts psychological properties in trouble with causal potency, why doesn't it put all other special-science properties, like chemical and biological properties, into the same sort of trouble? For the core of the supervenience argument apparently is the simple idea that if property P supervenes on base property P^*, P^* threatens to preempt the causal status of P. The argument is quite general and appears to have nothing to do with the fact that P is a mental property and P^* is a physical property. So if the argument works, it should work against the causal potency of all supervenient properties, and since there is good reason to believe that biological, geological, and other special-science properties are supervenient properties in the same sense in which mental properties are supervenient, the argument should work equally well against these properties. Granted that both the supervenient properties and their base properties are properties of the same objects and hence belong to the same ontological level, there still is the problem of *intralevel causal exclusion*. What we have shown is only that the causal exclusion problem is not an *interlevel* problem. I will return to this issue in my next lecture.[35]

Chapter 4

Reduction and Reductionism: A New Look

Expressions like "reduction," "reductionism," "reductionist theory," and "reductionist explanation" have become pejoratives not only in philosophy, on both sides of the Atlantic, but also in the general intellectual culture of today. They have become common epithets thrown at one's critical targets to tarnish them with intellectual naivete and backwardness. To call someone "a reductionist," in high-culture press if not in serious philosophy, goes beyond mere criticism or expression of doctrinal disagreement; it is to put a person down, to heap scorn on him and his work. We used to read about "bourgeois reductionism" in left-wing press; we now regularly encounter charges of "biological reductionism," "sociological reductionism," "economic reductionism," and the like, in the writings about culture, race, gender, and social class. If you want to be politically correct in philosophical matters, you would not dare come anywhere near reductionism, nor a reductionist. It is interesting to note that philosophers who are engaged in what clearly seem like reductionist projects would not call themselves reductionists or advertise their work as reductionist programs.[1] A general rehabilitation of the reductionist strategy is not something I would attempt—at least not here. What I want to do is to discuss how best to understand reduction in the sense that is relevant to our present concerns, what might motivate mind-body reductionism, and what its costs and benefits might be. I hope to persuade you that reductionism about the mind is a serious, motivated philosophical position, and that although in the end we may decide to reject it, we should do so for the right reasons. There is also some unfinished business to attend to in this final lecture—in particular, I need to say a bit more about what I called the generalization argument. As you may recall, this is the contention that the supervenience argument against mental causation and related considerations apply to all other special-science properties, and that this demonstrates the emptiness of the problem of mental causation. Our final consideration of the issue of the generalizability of the mental causation problem will lead us to some concluding reflections concerning what options are open to us in regard to the mind-body problem and mental causation.

Nagel Reduction: Troubles with "Bridge Laws"

Toward the end of my first lecture, I criticized Nagel's derivational model of theory reduction, especially its use in the debate over mind-body reductionism, and urged another way of looking at reduction, namely the functional model. As I noted, Nagel's model, although its limitations have been widely noted and many variants of it have been on the scene,[2] has dominated philosophical discussions of reduction and reductionism during the past three decades. At the heart of Nagel's model are "bridge laws," which provide the essential reductive links between the vocabulary of the theory targeted for reduction and that of the base theory, and thereby enable the derivation of the target theory from its reducer. In the philosophical applications of the model, it has been customary to assume these bridge laws to take the biconditional form, providing for each primitive predicate of the theory to be reduced with a nomologically coextensive predicate in the base theory. When the idiom in which reductionism was debated took a metaphysical turn and talk of properties became respectable again, the bridge-law requirement came to be understood as saying that each property in the domain to be reduced must be provided with a coextensive property (coextensive at least with nomic necessity) in the base domain.

Actually Nagel himself did not require that his bridge laws be biconditionals in form; his focus was on the derivability of the laws of the reduced theory from those of the base theory, and all he wanted was bridge laws in enough numbers and strength to enable the derivation. But this leaves the question of what bridge laws are needed dependent on the specific pairs of theories under consideration, and there is nothing general one can say about how the predicates of two theories, or properties in the domains of the two theories, must be related to each other to enable the reduction of one theory to the other. This means that unless we have two fixed and completed theories, we cannot really say anything useful about what bridge laws may be needed for reduction. As philosophers, however, we do want to discuss reducibility and reductionism before the final theories are in; in particular, in the mind-body case, neither psychology nor its putative reduction base, neurobiology or whatever, is anywhere near a finished form, and unlikely ever to get to that stage. Moreover it is obvious that the availability of bridge laws is the critical factor for questions about Nagel-reducibility of theories. In light of this the idea that bridge laws must be biconditionals makes excellent sense: if each predicate or property, M, in the target domain can be correlated with a coextension, P, in the base domain, that in itself would guarantee Nagelian reduction (assuming that both theories are true). For let L be any law of the theory being reduced: either L is derivable from the base theory via the biconditional bridge laws or it is not. If it is, Nagel reduction goes through for L. If it is not, rewrite L in the vocabulary of the base theory using the bridge laws as definitions, and add this rewrite as an additional law of the base theory. L would then be derivable from the laws of the enhanced based theory via the bridge laws, again satisfying Nagel's derivability condition. This rewrite of L is a true lawlike generalization expressed entirely in the vocabulary of the base theory, and the original theory was incomplete in that it missed a true generalization within its domain. Augmenting the base theory this way expands neither its ontology nor its ideology (that is, its system of concepts) and does not diminish in any way the scientific or philosophical interest of the reduction.[3]

Consider, then, bridge laws of the form $M \leftrightarrow P$, where M is a property in the target domain and P is a property in the base domain. I believe there are three important questions we need to consider concerning such laws.

(i) *The availability question.* This is the question raised explicitly by the multiple realization argument against type physicalism and later generalized by others to apply to all special-science properties.[4] The gist of this argument, which is by now familiar, is the observation that any higher-order property P has multiple realizers in lower-order properties, $Q_1, Q_2, \ldots$, so that it is not possible to provide P with a single lower-order correlate Q to yield a biconditional bridge law of the form $P \leftrightarrow Q$. Thus P is irreducible to some single lower-order property, and more generally, this shows that the requirement of biconditional bridge laws cannot be satisfied. That, at least, is the argument.

Davidson takes mental anomalism, in particular, his claim that there are no laws connecting mental and physical properties, to undermine mind-body reductionism. Under mental anomalism there cannot be any type of bridge laws between the mental and the physical, let alone biconditional ones. So, unlike Putnam's multiple realization argument, Davidson's argument doesn't depend on the assumption that bridge laws must be biconditionals. It is clear that considerations of multiple realizability do not show that there can be no laws connecting the two domains involved. In fact, if Q_i is a realizer of M, then $Q_i \rightarrow M$ must hold with nomological necessity. There is a further difference between Davidson's and Putnam's argument. As noted, the multiple realization argument seems quickly and naturally to generalize to other special-science properties outside psychology. However, Davidson's argument depends on mental anomalism, which in turn depends on the supposed special character of mental phenomena (specifically, propositional attitudes), namely their normativity and rationality. For this reason there is no reason to think that his argument can be generalized outside the mental domain. At any rate we will not consider Davidson's argument further here, for the following reason. For, as Davidson has lately emphasized,[5] his mental anomalism only denies the existence of what he calls "strict laws" between the mental and the physical, and on his understanding of strict law, it turns out that *there can be strict laws only in basic physics* (or, in Davidson's words, "developed physics"). Since Davidson bases his antireductive argument on mental anomalism, he must be requiring that the bridge laws used in a reduction must be strict laws. But, on his account, there aren't strict laws anywhere outside basic physics, from which it follows that there cannot be reduction anywhere in the sciences.[6] What this shows is that Davidson's idea of reduction is too narrow and unrealistic to be of much philosophical interest. If there is any reduction in science, the question whether there are strict bridge laws connecting the two domains involved (e.g., whether his mind-body anomalism is true) cannot be an issue of any relevance to reduction and reductionism.

There are two possible responses to the availability question raised by the multiple realizationists: (1) the disjunctive strategy and (2) the move to species- or structure-specific bridge laws and "local" reductions (as distinguished from "global" or "uniform" reductions).[7] The disjunctive strategy, briefly, is this: if M is multiply realizable in, say, three ways, P_1, P_2, and P_3, then why not take the disjunction, $P_1 \vee P_2 \vee P_3$, as M's coextension in the base domain? Clearly, given that each of the P_is is a realizer of M, it must hold with (at least) nomological necessity that $P_i \rightarrow M$, and given that the P_is are all the nomologically possible realizers of M, it must hold with (at least) nomological necessity that $M \leftrightarrow (P_1 \vee P_2 \vee P_3)$. But let us postpone discussion of the disjunction move (to a later section) and turn our attention to the idea of local reduction via species- or structure-specific bridge laws.

It is often a tacit supposition of the friends of the multiple realization argument that neural correlates of mental states, say pain, are species-specific—that pain is correlated with, and realized by, one neural state in humans, by a different neural state in octopuses, and perhaps by some electrochemical state in Martians. And this is understood to mean that if N_1 is pain's realizer in humans, the following biconditional restricted to humans holds: $H \rightarrow (\text{pain} \leftrightarrow N_1)$, where "H" stands for being a human. A pervasive system of these biconditionals covering all mental states in humans would enable a Nagelian derivational reduction of human psychology to, say, human neurobiology, and canine psychology to canine neurobiology, Martian psychology to Martian electrochemistry, and so on. It seems to me that from the general philosophical and methodological point of view that motivates the Nagelian model of reduction, these species-restricted, or "local," reductions are reduction enough. Given that the physical substrates for mentality differ for humans, canines, and Martians, what more could we expect or want, to begin with?

Three questions, however, can be raised concerning local reductions. The first, raised by a number of philosophers,[8] begins by pointing out that multiple realization goes deeper and wider than biological species, and that even in the same individual the neural realizer, or correlate, of a given mental state or function, may change over time through maturation and brain injuries. I think this is true, but the point, though it may be pragmatically relevant, is irrelevant from a metaphysical point of view. Presumably, if two conspecifics have different realizers for some single mental state, then that is so presumably because they differ in the organization of their neural systems. Maturation and injuries to the brain can cause changes in the basic neural substrates of our mental life, and that is why different neural states come to realize the same mental state over time. But conspecifics do share largely similar neural systems, and this is what makes psychology possible. It is a contingent, and fortunate, fact that human psychology is uniform enough to make its scientific investigation possible and practically worthwhile.[9] But the uniformity of human psychology, to the degree that it obtains, is due to the similarity in our neural systems—that is, the uniformity of human physiology. In the worst-case scenario in which there is wildly heterogeneous multiple realization everywhere among the humans, and for the same individual over time, there still would be *structure*-specific biconditional laws (if psychology is indeed physically realized), and there still would be perfectly good local reductions, even if they are only for single individuals at a particular moment of their lives. The idea that psychology is physically realized is the idea that it is the physical properties of the realizers of psychological states that generate psychological regularities and underlie psychological explanations. Given an extreme diversity and heterogeneity of realization, it would no longer be interesting or worthwhile to look for neural realizers of mental states for every human being at every moment of his/her existence. If psychology as a science were possible under these circumstances, that would be due to a massive and miraculous set of coincidences. We may conclude then that pushing multiple realizability to extremes does not impugn the idea of local reduction. It only makes local reductions more fine-grained and atomistic and perhaps renders them practically not worthwhile.

The second and third questions regarding local reductions are more serious and require substantive responses, not simple rebuttals. In fact these questions pose serious challenges to the whole idea of Nagel reduction and its appeal to bridge laws, not just to local reduction and species-specific bridge laws. Let us return to bridge laws in general and consider a pair of further questions.

(ii) *The explanatory question.* C-fiber stimulation correlates with pain (in all pain-capable organisms, or in humans and higher mammals—this makes no difference). But why? Can we understand why we experience pain when our C-fibers are firing, and not when our A-fibers are firing? Can we explain why pains, not itches or tickles, correlate with C-fiber firings? Exactly what is it about C-fibers and their excitation that explains the occurrence of a painful, hurting sensation? Why is any sensory quality experienced at all when C-fibers fire? When the emergentists claimed that consciousness was an emergent property that could not be explained in terms of its physical/biological "basal conditions," it was these explanatory questions that they despaired of ever answering. For them reduction was primarily, or at least importantly, an explanatory procedure: reduction must make intelligible how certain phenomena arise out of more basic phenomena, and if that is our goal, as I believe it should be, a Nagelian derivational reduction of psychology, with bridge laws taken as unexplained auxiliary premises, will not advance our understanding of mentality by an inch. *For it is the explanation of these bridge laws, an explanation of why there are just these mind-body correlations, that is at the heart of the demand for an explanation of mentality.* You will recall that we raised similar questions about mind-body supervenience (chapter 1); it is evident that the Nagel reduction of psychology is like taking mind-body supervenience as an unexplained brute fact.

I believe physicalists should take the explanatory question seriously. It isn't that on physicalism every phenomenon must be physically explainable; there may well be physical phenomena that aren't physically explainable—that is, this world may be a physical world but not fully physically explainable. Nor are we demanding that we actually succeed at some point in formulating a physical explanation of everything that can be explained. We may not be smart enough, diligent enough, or live long enough. But if a whole system of phenomena that are prima facie not among basic physical phenomena resists physical explanation, and especially if we don't even know where or how to begin, it would be time to reexamine one's physicalist commitments.

So Nagelian reductions, whether global or local, do not give us reductions that explain. Even if all phenomena have been Nagel-reduced to basic physical theory, of which let us suppose we have a completed version, the world would still be full of mysteries, mysteries that defy our completed physics.

(iii) *The ontological question.* It is arguably analytic that reduction must *simplify*; after all, reductions must reduce. We expect our reductions to yield simpler systems—a simpler system of concepts, or simpler system of assumptions, or simpler system of entities. On this score bridge laws of the form $M \leftrightarrow P$ apparently are wanting in various ways. Since $M \leftrightarrow P$ is supposed to be a contingent law, the concepts M and P remain distinct; hence bridge laws yield no conceptual simplification. Further, since we have only a contingent biconditional "iff" connecting properties

M and P, M and P remain distinct properties and there is no ontological simplification. The idea of local reduction appears to make the situation worse: there isn't even a single P that can be considered a candidate for identification with M, but a multitude of M's realizers, P_1, P_2, ... True, Nagel reduction gives us a simplified set of laws, through a derivational absorption of the laws of the reduced theory by the reducer. However, the simplicity so purchased may be largely illusory: the price paid is the addition of the bridge laws as new basic laws of the base theory, and moreover these laws, by bringing with them new descriptive terms, will expand both the language and ontology of the base theory. In any case the metaphysically significant fact is that Nagel reduction gives us no ontological simplification, and fails to give meaning to the intuitive "nothing over and above" that we rightly associate with the idea of reduction.

The philosophical poverty of a Nagel reduction of psychology to physical theory becomes evident when we reflect on the fact that nothing in emergentism, or many other forms of dualism such as the double-aspect theory, epiphenomenalism, and the doctrine of pre-established harmony, rules out a purely derivational reduction of psychology. Nor does substantival dualism as such preclude a Nagel reduction of psychology to physical theory. Moreover some of these dualist theories, for example, the double-aspect theory, *entail* the Nagel reducibility of psychology by providing us with all the mind-body bridge laws we need. We see therefore that the question whether or not mentality is Nagel-reducible via bridge laws to the physical cannot be a significant metaphysical issue. Nor can a refutation of reductionism that is premised on Nagelian reduction be considered a significant philosophical contribution.

The Functional Model of Reduction

If we want ontological simplification out of our reductions, we must somehow find a way of enhancing bridge laws, $M \leftrightarrow P$, into identities, $M = P$. (To simplify the discussion, we will for the moment ignore the issue of multiple realization and assume that M has a single correlate or realizer; we return to multiple realization later in this chapter.) A nice thing about these identities is that they serve to answer the explanatory question about bridge laws as well: M and P are coinstantiated because they are in fact one and the same property. Identity takes away the logical space in which explanatory questions can be formulated. To the question "Why is that whenever and wherever Hillary Rodham shows up, the President's wife also shows up?" there is no better, or conclusive, answer than "Hillary Rodham *is* the President's wife."

If M and P are both intrinsic properties and the bridge law connecting them is contingent, there is no hope of identifying them. Distinct properties are just distinct, and we can't pretend they are the same. I don't think it's good philosophy to say, as some materialists used to say, "But why can't we *just say* that they are one and the same? Give me good reasons why we shouldn't say that!" I think that we must try to provide positive reasons for saying that things that appear to be distinct are in fact one and the same. Moreover, if $M \leftrightarrow P$ is contingent, the identification of M with P must be made consistent with the thesis, defended by Kripke with great plausibility and now widely accepted, that identities whose terms are "rigid" are necessary. For if $M = P$ is necessary, $M \leftrightarrow P$ cannot be contingent—unless either M or P is nonrigid.

All this suggests that we should go back to the functional model of reduction described toward the end of my first lecture. To recapitulate: to reduce a property M to a domain of base properties, we must first "prime" M for reduction by construing, or reconstruing, it *relationally* or *extrinsically*. This turns M into a relational/extrinsic property. For functional reduction we construe M as a second-order property defined by its causal role—that is, by a causal specification H describing its (typical) causes and effects. So M is now the property of having a property with such-and-such causal potentials, and it turns out that property P is exactly the property that fits the causal specification. And this grounds the identification of M with P.[10] M is the property of having some property that meets specification H, and P is the property that meets H. So M is the property of having P. But in general the property of having property Q = property Q. It follows then that M is P.[11]

I have already given some examples of such functional reductions: the reduction of temperature and the gene (see chapter 1). A functional construal of the property to be reduced, M, serves as an explanation of why the $M \leftrightarrow P$ correlation holds and as a ground for the identity $M = P$, and it gives satisfying responses to both the explanatory and the ontological questions that arise for bare bridge laws unaccompanied by identities. I believe most cases of interlevel[12] reduction conform to the model I have just sketched. The crucial step in the process of course is the *functionalization* of the properties to be reduced. Indeed the possibility of functionalization is a necessary condition of reduction. As I have already said, if both M_i and P_i are distinct intrinsic properties in their own right, replacing $\leftrightarrow$ with = in the correlation $M_i \leftrightarrow P_i$ is entirely out of the question, and the correlation must be regarded as a brute fact that is not further explainable.

To functionalize M is to make M nonrigid, and this is easily seen: M is defined in terms of its causal/nomic relations to other properties, and since these relations are contingent—contingent on the laws that prevail in a given world—it is a contingent fact whether a given property satisfies the causal/nomic specification that is definitive of M.[13] This makes the realization relation vary from world to world, and the identity $M = P$ becomes metaphysically contingent. Does this lead to difficulties? Kripke has argued that such "theoretical" or reductive identities as "Heat is molecular motion" and "The gene is a DNA molecule" are metaphysically necessary.[14] Note, though, that on the functional model of reduction, $M = P$ is not wholly contingent: it is nomologically necessary. Since whether or not P is a realizer of the functional property M is determined by the prevailing laws of nature, the realization relation remains invariant across all worlds with the same basic laws. Thus $M = P$ holds in all nomologically possible worlds (in relation to the reference world). Accordingly we may say "M" is nomologically rigid or semi-rigid. This result seems right: given the prevailing laws, DNA-molecules are the carriers of genetic information in this world, but in worlds with different basic laws, it may well be molecules of another kind that perform this causal work. The upshot is that some theoretical identities, especially those arising out of functional reductions, are only nomologically necessary, not necessary *tout court*. We of course need not say that all reductive identities are only nomologically necessary; water = H_2O can remain metaphysically necessary, since we need not think of water, or being water, as a functional property.

The emergentists would have denied the functionalizability of the properties they claimed to be emergent. For them these properties are intrinsic properties in their own right, with their own distinctive causal powers that are irreducible to those of the processes from which they emerge. Their reason for thinking that the emergent relations are brute and unexplainable, or that emergents are irreducible to their "basal conditions," is often put in epistemic terms, to the effect that from a complete knowledge of the basal conditions, it is not possible to predict what properties will emerge at the higher level. For example, the emergentists early in this century argued that most chemical properties are emergent in this sense: from a complete knowledge of the hydrogen and the oxygen atoms in isolation, it is not possible to predict that when they bond in the ratio of 2 to 1, the resulting substance will be transparent and dissolve sugar but not copper. However, the emergentists were wrong about these examples: solid-state physics has explained, and is capable of predicting, these phenomena on the basis of microphysical facts.[15] I believe that the key to such explanation and prediction is the functional construal of the phenomenon, or property, to be explained. Consider the transparency of water: it would seem that once this property has been functionally understood, as the capacity of a substance to transmit light beams intact, there should be no in-principled obstacle to formulating a microphysical explanation of why H_2O molecules have this power. The same strategy should allow microphysical explanations and predictions of biological phenomena as well, for it seems that many biological properties seem construable as second-order functional properties over physicochemical properties.[16]

So the central question for us, in the mind-body debate, is this: Is the mental amenable to the kind of functionalization required for reductive explanation, or does it in principle resist such functionalization? If the functionalist conception of the mental is correct—correct for all mental properties—then mind-body reduction is in principle possible, if not practically feasible. This is contrary to one piece of current philosophical wisdom, the claim that functionalism, as distinguished from classic type physicalism, is a form—in fact the principal contemporary form—of mind-body antireductionism. What I am urging here is the exact opposite—that the functionalist conception of mental properties is *required* for mind-body reduction. In fact it is necessary and sufficient for reducibility. If this is right, mind-body reductionism and the functionalist approach to mentality stand or fall together; they share the same metaphysical fate.

It has been customary to distinguish between two broad categories of mental phenomena, the intentional and the phenomenal, without excluding those that have aspects of both (e.g., emotions). Intentionality is particularly evident in propositional attitudes—states carrying representational content. There has been much skepticism about the viability of a functionalist account of intentionality; in particular, Hilary Putnam, who introduced functionalism in the late 1960s, has recently mounted sustained attacks on the functionalist accounts of content and reference, and John Searle has also vigorously resisted the functionalization of intentionality.[17] However, like many others,[18] I remain unconvinced by these arguments; I don't see principled obstacles to a functional account of intentionality. Let me just say here that it seems to me inconceivable that a possible world exists that is an exact physical duplicate of this world but lacking wholly in intentionality.[19]

I am with those who believe that the main trouble comes from qualia. Unlike the case of intentional phenomena, we seem able, without much difficulty, to conceive an exact physical duplicate of this world in which qualia are distributed differently (worlds with qualia inversions) or entirely absent ("zombie worlds"), although the latter possibility is more controversial. To get to the point without fuss, it seems to me that the felt, phenomenal qualities of experiences, or qualia, are intrinsic properties if anything is.[20] To be sure, we commonly refer to them using extrinsic/causal descriptions like the color of jade, the smell of ammonia, or the taste of avocado. However, this is entirely consistent with the claim that what these descriptions pick out are intrinsic qualities, not something extrinsic or relational. (Perhaps it is because they are intrinsic and subjective that we need to resort to relational descriptions for intersubjective reference.) Compare our practice of ascribing intrinsic physical properties to material objects by the use of relational descriptions such as two kilograms or 32 degrees Fahrenheit. To say that an object has a mass of 2 kilograms is to say that it will balance, on an equal arm balance, two objects each of which would balance the Prototype Kilogram (an object stored somewhere in France, I believe). That is the linguistic meaning, or the concept if you prefer, of "2 kilograms;" however, the property it picks out, having a mass of 2 kilograms, is an intrinsic property of material bodies.

Why do I think that the functionalization of qualia won't work, while at the same time staying open-minded about intentionality? I obviously cannot open this much debated issue here, and I have nothing essentially new to offer. As noted, my doubts about the functionalist accounts of qualia are by and large based on the well-known, and not uncontested, arguments from qualia inversions and the familiar epistemic considerations. Further I find the following intuitive difference between qualia and intentionality significant: If someone should ask us to create a device with consciousness, say something that can feel pain, itch, tickle, and the like, the only thing we can do, it seems to me, is to make an appropriate duplicate of a structure, presumably a biological organism like a human or a cat, that we know, or believe, to be conscious and capable of these sensations. We are not capable of designing, through theoretical reasoning, a wholly new kind of structure that we can predict will be conscious; I don't think we even know how to begin, or indeed how to measure our success.

Whereas, if we are asked to design a structure that can perceive, process information received through perception, store it, make use of it to make inferences and guide action, and so on, we don't necessarily have to make a replica of a system that is known to do these things. It seems to me that we can go about designing— arguably we have already done so, in certain robots and com- puter-driven devices—wholly new sorts of structures with such capacities, devices that we can predict, on the basis of our theo- ries and their constructional detail, will have the capacity to perform these tasks. Evidently it is functionalizability that makes a critical difference here. In any case it seems to me that if emergentism is correct about anything, it is more likely to be correct about qualia than about anything else.

Functional Properties versus Functional Concepts

We must now confront the following question: if M is a second- order property and P a first-order property (or if M is an ex- trinsic/relational property and P an intrinsic one, or if M is a causal role and P is an occupant of that role), how could M be identical with P? Isn't it incoherent to think that a property could be both first-order and second-order, both extrinsic/ relational and intrinsic, both a role and its occupier?

So far we have been rather loose in our talk of properties, causal roles and their occupants, and the like. It is time to tidy up things a bit. I will now sketch a way of doing this. We may begin by explicitly recognizing that by existential quantification over a given domain of properties, we do not literally bring into being a new set of *properties*. That would be sheer magic, espe- cially if we adopt the plausible view that distinct properties must represent distinct causal powers. By mere logical operations on our notations, we cannot alter our ontology—we cannot dimin- ish or expand it. For something to have second-order property M is for it to have some first-order property or other meeting a certain specification. Say, there are three such first-order proper- ties, P_1, P_2, and P_3. For something to have M, then, is for it to have P_1 or have P_2 or have P_3. Here there is a *disjunctive proposition* or *fact* that the object has one or another of the three first-order properties; that is exactly what the fact that it has M amounts to. There is no need here to think of M itself as a property in its own right—not even a disjunctive property with the *P*s as disjuncts. By quantifying over properties, we cannot create new properties any more than by quantifying over individuals we can create new individuals.[21] Someone murdered Jones, and the murderer is Smith or Jones or Wang. That someone, who murdered Jones, is not a person in addition to Smith, Jones, and Wang, and it would be absurd to posit a disjunctive person, Smith-or-Jones-or-Wang, with whom to identify the murderer. The same goes for second-order properties and their realizers.

So it is less misleading to speak of second-order *descriptions* or *designators* of properties, or second-order *concepts*, than second-order properties. Second-order designators come in handy when we are not able or willing to name the properties we have in mind by the use of canonical first-order designators: so we say "having some property or other, P, such that . . . P . . .," instead of naming all the specific properties meeting the stated condition. The situation is the same when we are dealing with individuals: we say, "I shook hands with a Democratic senator at the reception yesterday," instead of saying "I shook hands with Claiborne Pell, or Ted Kennedy, or Patrick Moynahan, or . . ." (pretty soon you run out of names, or you may not even know any). Of course second-order designators also carry information that is valuable, perhaps indispensable in a given context, which is not conveyed by the canonical designators of the first-order realizers. We convey the information that we are talking about someone who is a Democratic senator, rather than, say, someone who owns a mansion in Newport or a family compound on Cape Cod. When we use the functional characterization of pain (that is, "pain" for the functionalist), we let others know that we are referring to a state with certain input-output properties; a neural characterization of its realizer, even if one is on hand, would in most ordinary contexts be useless and irrelevant. From the ordinary epistemic and practical point of view, the use of second-order property designators probably is unavoidable, and we should recognize that these designators introduce a set of useful and practically indispensable concepts that group first-order properties in ways that are essential for descriptive and communicative purposes. In building scientific theories, we hope that the concepts in our best theories pick out, or answer to, the real properties in the world. On the present view, the concepts introduced by second-order designators pick out first-order properties disjunctively. When I say, x has property M, where "M" is a second-order designator (or property, if you insist), "the truth-maker" of this statement is the fact, or state of affairs, that x has P_1 or P_2 or P_3, where the Ps are the realizers of M. (The "or" here is sentence disjunction, not predicate disjunction; it does not introduce disjunctive predicates with disjunctive properties as semantic values.) Suppose that in this particular case, x has M in virtue of having P_2, in which case the ultimate truth-maker of "x has M" is the fact that x has P_2. There is no further fact of the matter to the fact that x has M over and above the fact that x has P_2.

So I am advocating here what is called a "sparse" conception of properties as distinguished from the "latitudinarian" or "abundant" conception. An extreme form of the latter would regard every predicate as denoting, or representing, a property, with synonymy or logical equivalence taken as the condition under which two predicates denote the same property. On this conception of propertyhood, second-order predicates would indeed represent properties distinct from their first-order realizers. If anyone should insist, we should have no objection to these second-order properties as long as we are clear about the liberal conception of properties involved. I believe it is clear, although I will not belabor the point, that the conception of properties appropriate to the present context is the sparse one. In fact current debates over the mind-body problem and mental causation tacitly presuppose a particularly robust version of this approach according to which differences in properties must reflect differences in causal powers.[22] If synonymy is required for property identity, we should have thrown in the towel on the issue of reductionism a long time ago—when analytical behaviorism was generally acknowledged to have failed. Few problems that are now contested in discussions of the mind-body problem could even be intelligibly formulated in terms of the latitudinarian conception (for example, the problem of mental causation does not concern the causal efficacy of *psychological concepts*).

Let me briefly summarize the arguments of this section. A genuine explanatory reduction cannot be content with bridge laws assumed as unexplained premises of reductive derivations. For these are exactly what need to be explained. One way of satisfying the explanatory demand is to elevate the bridge laws to identities, and this can be done if the properties being reduced can be construed, or reconstrued, as causal/functional properties, second-order properties defined over the properties in the reduction base. And for a tidier ontological/conceptual landscape, we may want to, perhaps should, give up the talk of second-order properties altogether in favor of second-order designators of properties, or second-order concepts.[23]

Multiple Realization Again

The discussion thus far has assumed that the property M targeted for functional reduction has a single realizer. Let us now see how we may deal with the more realistic case where M has multiple realizers, say P_1 and P_2. The situation will not be altered in a significant way if there are an indefinitely many realizers.

Let us first suppose that we are serious about M as a property. I believe that this can be accomplished only if we are willing to countenance M as a disjunctive property, $P_1 \vee P_2$, but there are weighty reasons for rejecting disjunctive properties of this kind. The upshot, then, will be that we are in danger of losing M as a property, a property we will have to learn to live without.

To begin, if M is the property of having a property meeting a certain specification and P_1 and P_2 are all and only properties meeting this specification, then it seems obvious and trivial that having M is just having P_1 or P_2; there is no other way of having M.

(i) Having M = having P_1 or P_2.

But (i) doesn't imply the following (ii), and it is clearly prema-ture to think that the two say the same thing:

(ii) Property M = disjunctive property $P_1 \vee P_2$.

As we saw earlier, the reason is simply that the "or" in (i) is sentence disjunction. Thus what (ii) says is that the fact that something has M amounts to the fact that it has P_1 or it has P_2; it doesn't say that the fact that something's having M comes to its having a disjunctive property $P_1 \vee P_2$. At this point there is no reason to think that such a property exists, as the semantic value of the disjunctive predicate "has $P_1 \vee P_2$." And there is no reason to think that we have, or need, a disjunction as a predi-cate forming device. For most purposes the "or" that appears to disjoin predicates seems perfectly well understood as abbre-viating sentence disjunctions; thus "The ball is red or white" is short for "The ball is red or the ball is white," and the semantics of sentences like this does not require disjunctive properties, like being red $\vee$ white, any more than the sentence "She ate a hamburger or a hotdog" requires disjunctive snacks.

But why shouldn't we help ourselves with disjunctive proper-ties? If M can be saved only as a disjunctive property, perhaps that is good enough reason to allow disjunctive properties. I will not rehearse here the well-known general arguments against disjunctive properties.[24] These general arguments are fine as far as they go, but I don't think they go far enough, and moreover they depend excessively on intuitive judgments whose import is often not very clear. Instead, I'll present some considerations against disjunctive properties that are more directly appropriate to the present context.

Let us first consider disjunctive properties in a causal/explanatory context. Suppose that a certain medical symptom can be caused by two quite different pathological conditions. For example, both rheumatoid arthritis and lupus cause pains in the joints (or so I have heard). Suppose Mary has painful joints, and tests indicate that she has either lupus or rheumatoid arthritis, but we don't know which. Consider the following "deductive-nomological" argument (a "Hempelian" explanation):

Rheumatoid arthritis causes painful joints.
So does lupus.
Mary has either rheumatoid arthritis or lupus.
Therefore Mary has painful joints.

Do we have here an explanation of why Mary is experiencing pains in her joints? Do we know what is causing her pains? I think there is a perfectly clear and intelligible sense in which we don't as yet have an explanation: what we have is a *disjunction of two explanations*, not a *single disjunctive explanation*. What I mean is this: we have two possible explanations, and we know that one or the other is the correct one but not which it is. What we have, I claim, is not an explanation with a "disjunctive cause," having rheumatoid arthritis or lupus.[25] There are no such "disjunctive diseases."

At this point, one might object as follows: there are several types of lupus (as I understand it, lupus erythematosus and lupus vulgaris are the two principal types), so my point could be iterated for these subkinds of lupus, their subkinds, and so on, ad infinitum. My reply: if lupus erythematosus and lupus vulgaris are indeed different diseases, my point should apply to lupus as well. But that doesn't mean that it can be indefinitely iterated; not all subdivisions of a disease yield different diseases (for example, lupus in unemployed males and lupus in female government workers are not different diseases). And my point does not depend on there being an absolute, context-independent classificatory scheme for diseases. The point is that on whatever scheme of classification that is operative in a given context, disjunctions of diseases on that scheme will not automatically count, and usually will not count, as diseases in that context.

This point is related to a point I have argued elsewhere,[26] to the effect that the disjunction of heterogeneous properties can fail to be *projectible nomic properties*. I will briefly summarize the argument: suppose that we want to verify the "disjunctive law":

(D) Patients with either rheumatoid arthritis or lupus experience pains in their joints

and have accumulated numerous (say, one million) positive instances, that is, people who have one or the other disease and have painful joints, and no negative instances. Do these observations confirm the putative law? Not necessarily. For suppose that it turns out that all one million positive instances we have examined are exclusively persons with rheumatoid arthritis, and none with lupus. If this turns out to be the case, we would not, and should not, regard the putative disjunctive law as well confirmed. In fact this "law" is logically equivalent to the conjunction of the following two laws:

Patients with arthritis have painful joints

Patients with lupus have painful joints.

Our observed samples have nothing to do with the law about lupus and painful joints. If our data confirmed the disjunctive law, they should also confirm this second law, which is logically implied by it. So the disjunctive antecedent of the alleged law fails to be projectible and should not be considered a nomic kind. What we have in (D) is properly thought of as a conjunction of two laws, not a single law with a disjunctive antecedent. These reflections show the close associations that exist between ideas like being a *projectible nomic kind*, being a *kind of event*, and being *eligible as a cause* (thus, being citable as a *cause in a causal explanation*).

Thus, if we insist on having M as a disjunctive property, we may end up with a property that is largely useless. What good would it do to keep it as a property when it is not a projectible kind that can figure in laws, and cannot serve in causal explanations? Moreover there is a further related point to consider: Ex hypothesi, P_1 and P_2 are heterogeneous kinds, and if heterogeneity is going to mean anything significant, it must mean causal/nomic heterogeneity. Now, any instance of M must be either a P_1-instance or a P_2-instance, and this means that instances of M are not going to show the kind of causal/nomological homogeneity we expect from a scientific kind. In short, multiply realizable properties are causally and nomologically heterogeneous kinds, and this at bottom is the reason for their inductive unprojectibility and ineligibility as causes.[27]

I believe these considerations strengthen the case made earlier for eschewing the talk of functional *properties* in favor of functional *concepts* and *expressions*. What lends unity to the talk of dormitivity and such is conceptual unity, not the unity of some underlying property. Qua property, dormitivity is heterogeneous and disjunctive, and it lacks the kind of causal homogeneity and projectibility that we demand from kinds and properties useful in formulating laws and explanations. But dormitivity may well serve important conceptual and epistemic needs, by grouping properties that share features of interest to us in a given context of inquiry.

So where does all this leave us as regards reduction and reductionism? Let M be a mental property (or any other property in consideration for reduction), and let us suppose how we should view the situation when the functional model of reduction is brought to bear on M (and its cohort). A functional reduction of M requires the functionalization of M; let us assume that this has been done. We also assume that M has multiple physical realizers in different species and structures and can have different realizers in different possible worlds. The reduction consists in identifying M with its realizer P_i relative to the species or structure under consideration (also relative to the reference world). Thus M is P_1 in species 1, P_2 in species 2, and so on. Given that each instance of M has exactly the causal powers of its realizer on that occasion ("the causal inheritance principle"), all the causal/explanatory work done by an instance of M that occurs in virtue of the instantiation of realizer P_1 is done by P_1, and similarly for other instances of M and their realizers. In fact each instance of M is an instance of P_1, or of P_2, or . . . , where the Ps are M's realizers. This contrasts with Nagelian reduction via bridge laws in which M only nomologically correlates with P_1 in species 1 but remains distinct from it, and similarly for P_2, and so on.

In this way multiply realized properties are sundered into their diverse realizers in different species and structures, and in different possible worlds. To those who want to hang onto them as unified and robust properties in their own right, this no doubt comes as a disappointment. But I believe that the conclusion to which we have been led is inescapable, as long as we accept the causal inheritance principle and seriously believe in multiple realization.[28]

Before concluding this section let us briefly consider how the explanatory question is answered by functionalist reduction in the context of multiple realization. You may recall that we found Nagel reduction to fall short as explanatory reduction on account of its failure to explain the bridge laws—that is, explain why M occurs just when P occurs, where $M \leftrightarrow P$ is a bridge law. When I dealt with this question in regard to functional reduction, I said that if P is M's unique realizer, the functional reduction of M to P motivates identification of M with P, and that this solves the explanatory question. Now the situation of course is different if M has multiple distinct realizers—say, P_1 and P_2—since the identification of M with either P_1 or P_2 is out of the question. And we saw some pitfalls in recognizing the disjunctive property $P_1 \vee P_2$ with which to identify M. I also urged that M be viewed as a concept, not a property in the world; however, this is to duck the issue—we need a more straightforward answer. So what should we say about the explanatory question if we are to recognize M as a property with multiple realizers, P_1 and P_2? I believe there are perfectly satisfying answers to various explanatory questions that can be raised about the relationship between M and P_1 (or P_2). Why does a system s instantiate M at t? Because it is instantiating P_1 at t, and P_1 is a realizer of M in systems of the kind that s is—that is, having M is, by definition, to have some property with causal specification H and in systems like s, P_1 meets specification H. Why do these systems instantiate M not M^*

whenever they instantiate P_1? Because in systems like these, P_1 is a realizer of M but not of M^*. And so on. It seems to me clear that these are satisfying answers, and that to answer the explanatory question it is not necessary for functional reduction to yield general property identities.

The Supervenience Argument Revisited

In the third lecture, as you may recall, I left the generalization argument without a final resolution. To refresh your memory, the generalization argument is intended to show that the problem of mental causation is nothing to worry about because the same considerations lead to exactly parallel problems for all special science properties, not just psychological properties. The part of this argument that has been left unresolved is this: in my second lecture, I tried to generate a problem for mental causation from the doctrine of mind-body supervenience—this was the supervenience argument. The objection to this argument to which I need to respond, then, runs as follows: the supervenience argument seems to exploit only the fact or assumption of mind-body supervenience, having nothing to do with any special characteristic of the mental or of the physical. Consider now special-science properties like biological and chemical properties: these too supervene on basic physical properties—in fact there is even stronger reason to believe in supervenience for these properties than for mental properties (after all, there is still no consensus on whether qualia supervene on the physical). But there seems to be no particular problem about biological causation or chemical causation—causal relations involving biological or chemical properties; hence the supervenience of X on physical properties cannot generate difficulties for the causal efficacy of X, and this clearly applies to mental properties. This is the core of the generalization argument, something that still needs to be dealt with.

I will approach the issues somewhat obliquely. Let us begin by considering the idea of a physical property—what makes a property a physical property. In raising this question, I am not seeking a definition or a general criterion. The question I am interested in is rather this: Assuming that the usual properties and magnitudes that figure in our basic physics are physical properties, what other properties are to be counted as belonging to the physical domain? When we speak of physical properties in discussing the mind-body problem, we standardly include chemical, biological, and neural properties among physical properties as part of the physical domain. Without invoking a general criterion of what counts as physical and what counts as nonphysical, can we give some principled ground for this practice? And when we speak of the causal closure of the physical domain, just what is being included in the physical domain, and why? We assume that the properties of basic physics are in this domain, but what else gets in there and why?

There is a tendency among antireductionist philosophers, especially those who invoke the generalization argument to escape the problem of mental causation, to construe the physical domain excessively narrowly, without good reason. Perhaps the standard micro-macro hierarchical model encourages the idea that the causally closed physical domain includes only the basic particles and their properties and relations. But this is a groundless assumption. Plainly the physical domain must also include aggregates of basic particles, aggregates of these aggregates, and so on, without end; atoms, molecules, cells, tables, planets, computers, biological organisms, and all the rest must be, without question, part of the physical domain. What then of properties? What properties, in addition to the properties and relations of basic particles, are to be allowed into the physical domain—that is, to be counted among physical properties? Obviously mass of one kilogram should be allowed in, although no basic particle has this property, aggregates of basic particles can have this property, and it clearly is a physical property.

But why is having a mass of one kilogram a physical property? Perhaps it's silly to ask this question, but there is an answer that may be instructive: because it is a micro-based property whose constituents are physical properties and relations. We can think of this property as the property of being made up of proper parts, a_i, each with a mass of m_i, where the ms sum to one kilogram. And it seems appropriate to assume that the physical domain is closed under formation of micro-based properties: if P is a micro-based property of having parts $a_1, \ldots, a_n$, such that $P_1(a_1), \ldots, P_n(a_n)$, and $R(a_1, \ldots, a_n)$, then P is a physical property provided that $P_1, \ldots, P_2$, and R are physical properties (and relations), and each a_i is a basic particle or an aggregate of basic particles.

On this understanding, being a water molecule is a physical property, and being composed of water molecules (that is, being water) is also a physical property. It is important that these micro-based properties are counted as physical, for otherwise the physical domain won't be causally closed. Having a mass of one kilogram has causal powers that no smaller masses have, and water molecules, or the property of being water, have causal powers not had by individual hydrogen and oxygen atoms.

Are there other properties to be allowed in? Consider second-order properties. Given our discussion thus far of second-order properties and their realizers, it seems entirely proper to count as physical any second-order property defined over physical properties. Thus, if **D** is a set of physical properties, any property defined over **D** by existential quantification, in the manner of "the property of having some property P in **D** such that $H(P)$," where "H" specifies a condition on members of **D**, is also a physical property. Something further perhaps needs to be said about the vocabulary in which the condition H is specified, but we may assume that causal and nomological concepts belong in the permissible vocabulary.[29] If so, functional properties over physical properties count as physical. I earlier recommended that we give up talk of second-order *properties* in favor of second-order *property designators*. If this recommendation is accepted, the closure condition on second-order properties may be appropriately rephrased so that it applies to property designators—what is to count as a physical property designator.

We therefore have three closure conditions on the physical domain: first, any entity aggregated out of physical entities is physical; second, any property that is formed as micro-based properties in terms of entities and properties in the physical domain is physical; third, any property defined as a second-order property over physical properties is physical. Are there other closure conditions? I am not sure. Conjunctive properties, if we want to allow them, may be handled as a special case of micro-based properties (if we waive the condition that the constituents of a micro-based property must be *proper* constituents): the property of having P & Q is the property of being composed of parts a_1 and a_2, where $a_1 = a_2$ such that a_1 is P and a_2 is Q.[30] But disjunction and complementation (negation) are not in yet; as we saw with disjunctive properties, these operations give rise to some complicated considerations that we need not go into for the present purposes.

What we have is enough to let in chemical properties. So-called dispositional properties seem to get in either as second-order properties or micro-based properties. If transparency is taken as the property of passing light beams through without altering them, it counts as a second-order functional property. If transparency is identified with some microstructure, it will qualify as a micro-based property. The same can be said of such properties as water-solubility, ductility, thermal conductivity, inflammability, and the like. How about biological properties? Without going into details, I believe they behave like chemical properties: they qualify as physical in virtue of one or the other of two closure rules on physical properties. Being a cell may be a micro-based property; being a heart may be a second-order functional property (i.e., being a heart is plausibly viewed as being an organ/device with powers to pump blood). But being the kind of physical/biological structure that a human heart is may be a micro-based property. Actually the distinction between micro-based and functional properties is probably not sharp or absolute; for example, there surely can be micro-based properties some of whose constituent properties are functional properties.

As we saw earlier (chapter 2), functional properties, as second-order properties, do not bring new causal powers into the world: they do not have causal powers that go beyond the causal

powers of their first-order realizers. According to the causal
inheritance principle,[31] the causal powers of an instance of a
second-order property are identical with (or a subset of) the
causal powers of the first-order realizer that is instantiated on
that occasion. This means that second-order properties represent
heterogeneous causal powers, but none that go beyond the
causal powers of the first-order properties already in our domain
over which they are defined. There are therefore no special problems about the causal powers of functional properties. And if
any mental properties turn out to be functional properties, there
are no special problems about their causal roles either. This fits
nicely with the model of reduction we have urged: reduction is
essentially functionalization, and if the mental is reduced to the
physical, we should expect no special problem about its causal
powers. As we just saw, the functionalization of mental properties enables them to escape the supervenience argument.
According to the view being urged here, functional mental properties turn out, on account of their multiple realization, to be
causally heterogeneous but not causally impotent. This solves
the problem of causal efficacy for functionalizable mental properties. It is those mental properties that resist functionalization
that present difficulties when we try to give an account of their
causal powers. So long as we think there possibly are nonfunctionalizable mental properties, for example, qualia, which nonetheless supervene on physical properties, we are faced with the
problem of mental causation.

What of the causal powers of micro-based physical properties?
These properties are, by their construction, supervenient on
configurations of more basic, lower-level physical properties and
relations. And if we assume that properties are primarily individuated in terms of causal powers, we must also consider their
causal powers to be supervenient in the same way. But
mereological supervenience is not mereological reduction of
causal powers to those of their parts: the causal powers of the
supervening property P may be *fixed*, or *determined*, by the causal
powers of the properties and relations, $P_1, \ldots, P_2, R$, that figure

in P's construction as a micro-based property, but they need not be, and are not likely to be, *identical* with the causal powers of these constituent properties and relations. There is a world of difference between *determination* and *identity*.[32] Moreover we must distinguish both determination and identity from *explainability*. It may be that the causal powers of a micro-based property may be determined by its microstructural details but we may not be able to explain—in fact there may be no explanation of—why a property so microconstituted should have just these causal powers. This would be another way in which a macro-property may be emergent. Further the fact that we can microstructurally explain why a micro-based property has a certain set of causal powers does not mean that these causal powers are identical with the causal powers of its micro-constituents. Micro-reductively explainable causal powers may be new causal powers, net additions to the causal structure of the world. None of this is in conflict with the basic commitments of physicalism. Physicalism need not be, and should not be, identified with micro-physicalism.

This means that the case of micro-based properties is not at all parallel to the case of supervenient psychological properties. In the latter case the physical base properties, presumably certain neurobiological properties, are at the same level as the psychological properties: they are both had by human beings and other sentient creatures. This is part of what generates the problem about mental causation: the causal role of a mental property had by me is threatened with preemption by another property, a neural property, also had by me. My causal powers seem fully explicable not only *in terms of* but also *as* the causal powers of my neural/biological/physical properties.

Difficulties of this sort do not arise for micro-based properties in relation to their constituent properties because the former do not supervene on the latter taken individually or as a group. Rather, they supervene on *specific mereological configurations* involving these microproperties—for a rather obvious and uninteresting reason: they *are* identical with these micro-configurations. Now it is an interesting question whether or not the causal powers of a given micro-based property can be calculated, or predicted, on the basis of the causal powers of its micro-constituents and the way they are configured. This is another side of the question of explainability alluded earlier, and it is closely tied to the debate on property emergence. There is more to be said about micro-based properties, their causal powers, and the status of scientific theories about them, but we must move on.[33]

It follows then that we must grant novel causal powers to micro-based properties at higher levels—novel in the sense that these causal powers are not had by any lower-level properties that constitute them. And, as we saw, the supervenience argument does not apply to them, and their causal roles are not threatened by the supervenience argument.

What all this means is that the supervenience argument would generalize only to those nonmental properties, if any, that are supervenient on other properties (at the same level) but that resist functionalization in terms of their base properties. And as noted, the argument does not apply to micro-based properties. If we think of functionalization as reduction, as I recommended, the problem of mental causation generalizes to supervenient properties that are not reducible to their base properties.

The Options: Good News and Bad News

This gives us stark choices. If we are prepared to go for a functionalization of all mental properties, we will be embracing an all-encompassing reductionism about the mental, and this will solve the problem of mental causation. That's the good news. On a reductionist position of this sort, however, the causal powers of mental properties turn out to be just those of their physical realizers, and there are no new causal powers brought into the world by mental properties. Many will consider that bad news. But the real bad news is that some mental properties, notably phenomenal properties of conscious experiences, seem to resist functionalization, and this means that there is no way to account for their causal efficacy within a physicalist scheme. These properties are not able to overcome the supervenience argument.

If we hold out on functionalization for at least a selected group of mental properties, we come to a choice point with two branches: you take the first branch if you want to stay with physicalism (at least to the extent of respecting the physical causal closure), and take the second if you decide to abandon physicalism in favor of a serious form of dualism (you will need at least to abandon mind-body supervenience, and may have to consider substantival dualism as a serious option). Going back to the physicalist branch, if you stay with physicalism, you come to another choice point: either you retain supervenient and yet irreducible (that is, nonfunctionalizable) mental properties, say qualia, but accept their causal impotence, or you embrace mental eliminativism and deny the reality of these irreducible properties. Either way you lose—again, bad news.

The bad news continues: there may really be not much difference between these two options, eliminativism and epiphenomenalism. For a plausible criterion for distinguishing what is real from what is not real is the possession of causal power. As Samuel Alexander said, something that "has nothing to do, no purpose to serve"—that is, something with no causal power— "might as well, and undoubtedly would in time, be abolished."[34] So on Alexander's criterion of what is real, eliminativism and epiphenomenalism both come to pretty much the same thing: mental irrealism. But one might ask: Is the reductionist option much better? Doesn't it lead to the conclusion that the mental has no distinctive role of its own, having been entirely absorbed into the physical domain? That again may seem to some as a form of mental irrealism, and one might think it makes no sense to save mental causation while relinquishing mentality as a distinctive reality.[35] So the only piece of good news may turn into just more bad news. So all roads branching out of physicalism may in the end seem to converge at the same point, the irreality of the mental. This should come as no surprise: we should remember that physicalism, as an overarching metaphysical doctrine about all of reality, exacts a steep price. I don't know how to convince you of this, but it seems clear to me that preserving the mental as part of the physical world is far better than epiphenomenalism or outright eliminativism.

At any rate, what is becoming increasingly clear from the continuing debate over the mind-body problem is that currently popular middle-of-the-road positions, like property dualism, anomalous monism, and nonreductive physicalism, are not easily tolerated by robust physicalism. To think that one can be a serious physicalist and at the same time enjoy the company of things and phenomena that are nonphysical, I believe, is an idle dream. Reductive physicalism saves the mental but only as a part of the physical. If what I have argued in these lectures is in the right ballpark, that is what we should expect from physicalism. And that is what we should have expected all along. Physicalism cannot be had on the cheap.

It will be premature, however, to conclude that an all-out dualism offers a more realistic chance of saving the mental. For most of us, dualism is an uncharted territory, and we have little knowledge of what possibilities and dangers lurk in this dark cavern.[36]

Notes

Chapter 1

1. Herbert Feigl, "The 'Mental' and the 'Physical'," *Minnesota Studies in the Philosophy of Science,* vol. 2, ed. Herbert Feigl, Grover Maxwell, and Michael Scriven (Minneapolis: University of Minnesota Press, 1958). J. J. C. Smart, "Sensations and Brain Processes," *Philosophical Review* 68 (1959): 141–156.
2. U. T. Place, "Is Consciousness a Brain Process?" Part I, *British Journal of Psychology* 47 (1956): 44–50.
3. Gilbert Ryle, *The Concept of Mind* (London: Hutchinson, 1949). Ludwig Wittgenstein, *Philosophical Investigations,* trans. G. E. M. Anscombe (Oxford: Blackwell, 1953). C. D. Broad, *The Mind and Its Place in Nature* (London: Routledge and Kegan Paul, 1925).
4. In "Psychological Predicates," first published in 1968 and later reprinted under the title "The Nature of Mental States," in Hilary Putnam, *Collected Papers* II (Cambridge: Cambridge University Press, 1975). The argument, briefly, is that mental states can, and do, have vastly diverse physical/biological realizations in different species and structures (for example, the neural realizer of pain in humans presumably is quite different from its realizer in mollusks) and, in consequence, that no mental state can be identified with any (single) physical/biological state. For more details, see my "Multiple Realization and the Metaphysics of Reduction," reprinted in *Supervenience and Mind* (Cambridge: Cambridge University Press, 1993).
5. In "Mental Events," first published in 1970 and reprinted in Davidson, *Essays on Actions and Events* (Oxford: Oxford University Press, 1980).
6. One of Davidson's early papers on anomalous monism carries the title "Psychology as Philosophy" (reprinted in his *Essays on Actions and Events*). This presumably was meant to contrast with "psychology as a science."
7. What some philosophers take to be token physicalism appears to differ from Davidson's monism. Their token physicalism identifies *mental property instances* with *physical property instances,* where an "instance" of property F is like a trope of F (or an F-exemplification as an event, à la the theory of events as property exemplifications), rather than something (an event, object) that has or instantiates F. This form of token physicalism is, in fact,

rather like what I have called "multiple-type physicalism" in *Supervenience and Mind*, pp. 364ff.

8. *Essays on Actions and Events*, p. 214.
9. In fact there is a question whether the anomalism of the mental is consistent with mind-body supervenience. It is arguable that any supervenience relation that can support a claim of dependence of the supervenient on the subvenient must be some form of "strong supervenience" (see below), and that the strong supervenience of the mental on the physical is inconsistent with the denial of lawlike connections between the two domains. For further details, see my "Concepts of Supervenience" in *Supervenience and Mind* (Cambridge: Cambridge University Press, 1993). Davidson himself later opted for "weak supervenience" (see his "Thinking Causes," in *Mental Causation*, ed. John Heil and Alfred Mele, Oxford: Clarendon, 1993, p. 4n.4). This makes his supervenience claim consistent with his anomalism; however, it throws in doubt his claim of mental-physical dependence.
10. On the ambiguous metaphysical stance of functionalism concerning the mind-body problem, see Ned Block's "Introduction: What Is Functionalism?" in *Readings in Philosophy of Psychology*, vol. 1, ed. Block (Cambridge: Harvard University Press, 1980). It is interesting to note that some functionalists (such as David Armstrong and David Lewis) thought they were defending type physicalism, whereas others (such as Putnam and Fodor) thought they were refuting it.
11. The first philosophical use of this term (roughly in its current sense) that I know of is in Hilary Putnam's "Minds and Machines," in *Dimensions of Mind*, ed. Sydney Hook (New York: New York University Press, 1960).
12. In his "Anti-Reductionism Slaps Back," *Philosophical Perspectives* 11 (1997): 107–132.
13. I have argued elsewhere that classic emergentism is appropriately taken as the first articulation of nonreductive physicalism. See my "The Nonreductivist's Troubles with Mental Causation," in *Supervenience and Mind* (Cambridge: Cambridge University Press, 1993).
14. See, for example, John R. Searle, *The Rediscovery of the Mind* (Cambridge: MIT Press, 1992). Another sign of new interest in emergence is the recent volume of essays on emergence, *Emergence or Reduction?* ed. Ansgar Beckermann, Hans Flohr, and Jaegwon Kim (Berlin: De Gruyter, 1992).
15. For example, Francisco Varela, Evan Thompson, and Eleanor Rosch, *The Embodied Mind* (Cambridge: MIT Press, 1993). See especially part IV entitled "Varieties of Emergence." At the time of this writing, I know of two new volumes of papers on emergence, mostly by scientists from various disciplines, that are being prepared for publication in Europe (in France and Denmark). The topic of the 1997 Oberlin Philosophy Colloquium was "Emergence and Reductionism."
16. I give emergence fuller discussion in "Making Sense of Emergence," forthcoming in *Philosophical Studies*.

17. David Lewis, "New Work for a Theory of Universals," *Australasian Journal of Philosophy* 61 (1983): 343–377.

18. Or, if you have qualms about their equivalence, it is safe enough to assume that anyone who accepts one would also accept the other. For more details on this issue, see my "'Strong' and 'Global' Supervenience Revisited," reprinted in *Supervenience and Mind,* and Brian McLaughlin, "Varieties of Supervenience," in *Supervenience: New Essays,* ed. E. Savellos and Umit D. Yalcin (Cambridge: Cambridge University Press, 1995). McLaughlin's essay is a comprehensive and useful survey and analysis of supervenience concepts—an indispensable guide to supervenience.

19. See, for example, John Post, *The Faces of Existence* (Ithaca: Cornell University Press, 1987), and my "Supervenience as a Philosophical Concept" in *Supervenience and Mind.*

20. Mind-body supervenience is not excluded even by substance dualism.

21. On the need for explaining supervenience relations, see Terence Horgan, "Supervenience and Cosmic Hermeneutics," *Southern Journal of Philosophy* 22, suppl. (1984), 19–38, and Terence Horgan and Mark Timmons, "Troubles on Moral Twin Earth: Moral Queerness Revisited," *Synthese* 92 (1992): 221–260; Horgan, "From Supervenience to Superdupervenience," *Mind* 102 (1993): 555–586. As far as I know, Horgan was the first to stress why it is important for the physicalist to give a physicalist account of mind-body supervenience. Also it was Horgan who first suggested the functionalizability of mental properties as a possible explanation of their supervenience; see the paper by Horgan and Timmons cited above.

22. There are forms of dualism, for example, Spinozistic double-aspect theory and Leibniz's doctrine of preestablished harmony, that are consistent with supervenience as property covariation but not with full-fledged supervenience that includes asymmetric dependence. We may also note that although emergentism appears to be committed to mind-body supervenience, it is by no means clear that another of its basic tenets, namely the doctrine of "downward causation," is consistent with the supervenience thesis. See my "'Downward Causation' in Emergentism and Nonreductive Physicalism," in *Emergence or Reduction?,* ed. A. Beckermann, H. Flohr, and J. Kim (Berlin: De Gruyter, 1992).

23. The layered model as such of course does not need to posit a bottom level; it is consistent with an infinitely descending series of levels.

24. In his work on vision David Marr famously distinguishes three levels of analysis: the computational, the algorithmic, and the implementational. See his *Vision* (New York: Freeman Press, 1982). The emergentists, early in this century, appear to have been first to give an explicit formulation of the layered model; for example, see C. Lloyd Morgan, *Emergent Evolution* (London: Williams and Norgate, 1923). For a particularly clear and useful statement of the model, see Paul Oppenheim and Hilary Putnam, "Unity of

Science as a Working Hypothesis," *Minnesota Studies in the Philosophy of Science*, vol. 2 (1958).

25. Although a bit too restrictive; see my "Supervenience for Multiple Domains," reprinted in *Supervenience and Mind*.

26. If we assume that there is a bottom level, everything will have a unique decomposition into bottom-level entities, and the following should be provable: if x and y are micro-indiscernible with respect to their decompositions into bottom-level entities, they are micro-indiscernible.

27. We will leave the modal force of this claim unspecified. Depending on the modality one favors (nomological, metaphysical, conceptual, etc.), different versions of physical realizationism will emerge. The discussion to follow is by and large independent of this issue.

28. Standard versions of functionalism would also include mental states in the outputs; for example, in the case of pain such mental states as a sense of distress and a desire to be rid of it. For expository simplicity we ignore this complication here.

29. Hilary Putnam is responsible for both the functionalist conception of mentality and the general idea of a second-order property. On the latter see his "On Properties," in *Philosophical Papers*, vol. 1 (Cambridge: Cambridge University Press, 1975). Given that the father of functionalism also introduced the notion of second-order property, it is ironic that this notion did not enter the discussion of functionalism until Ned Block began using it in, for example, "Can the Mind Change the World?" in *Meaning and Method*, ed. George Boolos (Cambridge: Cambridge University Press, 1990). In "On Properties," however, Putnam did not explicitly relate the notion of realization to that of second-order property.

30. Of course one might develop a sort of foundationalist argument to show that if there are second-order properties, there must be properties that are first-order in some absolute sense.

31. Whether relational/historical properties are to be included can become an issue if wide-content properties are to be construed as second-order functional properties. Also we need not exclude nonphysical properties from the base domain: if physical realizationism is correct, no nonphysical properties will be realizers of mental properties.

32. Alternatively, having a primary color can be defined as follows: having some P in the set of colors such that P is a member of a minimal set of colors such that every color can be produced by adding members of this set. As it turns out, the second-order property defined this way has the same realizers as the property defined in the text. Does this mean that the two properties are in fact one and the same? The discussion to follow has certain consequences for this question.

33. More precisely speaking, all properties P such that P is the property of being mineral M, for every mineral kind M. To avoid verbosity, we will often use the simpler terminology.

34. To borrow an example from Block, "Can the Mind Change the World?"
35. Here we must skirt various complex issues about properties: what "intrinsic" and "extrinsic" mean for properties, whether the intrinsic/extrinsic distinction is absolute or relative, whether realizers of a functional property can themselves be second-order (relative to another domain), and so on. The hope of course is that we don't need to resolve all these issues before we can use the concepts involved for our present purposes.
36. See also my "Multiple Realization and the Metaphysics of Reduction," reprinted in *Supervenience and Mind*.
37. Unless we have in mind "total realizers" in something like Sydney Shoemaker's sense. See his helpful distinction between "core realization" and "total realization," in "Some Varieties of Functionalism," reprinted in *Identity, Cause, and Mind* (Cambridge: Cambridge University Press, 1984). See also Ronald Endicott, "Constructival Plasticity," *Philosophical Studies* 74 (1994): 51–75. The discussion here assumes that input and output specifications are held constant for all systems, which is a highly idealized (in fact evidently false) assumption. Surely what counts as pain input or pain output, from a purely physical point of view, differs greatly for different species (say, humans and octopuses), and is likely to show significant differences even among humans.
38. This discussion assumes that individuation of properties is independent of the laws in which they figure. This assumption is at least debatable, but a proper discussion of the issues involved is likely to be highly complex and must be set aside.
39. This therefore is in opposition to the claim associated with Saul Kripke that such reductive identities are metaphysically necessary; see his *Naming and Necessity* (Harvard: Cambridge University Press, 1980). The difference derives from the fact that I construe "temperature" and the like as nonrigid designators (in Kripke's sense). These terms are referentially stable only across nomologically possible worlds; we may call them "semi-rigid" or "nomologically rigid."
40. See *The Structure of Science* (New York: Harcourt, Brace & World, 1961), ch. 11.
41. See J. A. Fodor, "Special Sciences, or the Disunity of Science as a Working Hypothesis," *Synthese* 28 (1974): 97–115.
42. In particular, outside technical discussions in philosophy of science.
43. There are procedures called "reduction" in the sciences that appear to consist simply, or chiefly, in derivations, for example, the "reduction" of Kepler's laws of planetary motion to Newtonian mechanics and law of gravitation, the "reduction" of Newtonian physics to relativistic physics by taking certain parameters to assume, or approach, certain extremal values. Note, however, that none of these cases involve Nagelian bridge laws in a nontrivial sense.

Notes to Chapter 2

1. For Pierre Gassendi's vigorous challenge to Descartes, see René Descartes, *The Philosophical Writings of Descartes*, vol. 2, ed. John Cottingham, Robert Stoothoff, and Dugald Murdoch (Cambridge: Cambridge University Press, 1985), p. 238.
2. "Making Mind Matter More," reprinted in *A Theory of Content and Other Essays* (Cambridge: MIT Press, 1990), p. 156.
3. Davidson, "Mental Events," reprinted in *Essays on Actions and Events* (Oxford: Oxford University Press, 1980). For wholly different considerations in favor of mental anomalism, see Norman Malcolm, *Memory and Mind* (Ithaca: Cornell University Press, 1977), and Bruce Goldberg, "The Correspondence Hypothesis," *Philosophical Review* 77 (1968): 439–454.
4. This condition is not as widely accepted as it used to be. All known alternatives have their own difficulties, however, and it is fair to say that the nomological conception of causation, in its many variants, is still "the received view."
5. To cite a few of the papers in which this issue has been raised, Frederick Stoutland, "Oblique Causation and Reasons for Action," *Synthese* 43 (1980): 351–367; Ted Honderich, "The Argument for Anomalous Monism," *Analysis* 42 (1982): 59–64; Ernest Sosa, "Mind-Body Interaction and Supervenient Causation," *Midwest Studies in Philosophy* 9 (1984): 271–281; Jaegwon Kim, "Self-understanding and Rationalizing Explanations," *Philosophia Naturalis* 82 (1984): 309–320; Louise Antony, "Anomalous Monism and the Problem of Explanatory Force," *Philosophical Review* 98 (1989): 153–187. Davidson defends his position in "Thinking Causes," in *Mental Causation,* ed. John Heil and Alfred Mele (Oxford: Clarendon, 1993). This volume also includes rejoinders to Davidson by Kim, Sosa, and Brian McLaughlin.
6. This remains true even if Davidson's "strict law" requirement on causation is weakened so that nonstrict laws (or *ceteris paribus* laws)—including nonstrict psychophysical laws—are allowed to support causal relations. For suppose that m falls under mental kind M and that there is a nonstrict law connecting M with P (or another physical kind P^* under which p falls). Might this show M to be efficacious in m's causation of p? Hardly, for given that m's causation of p is covered by the strict law connecting N and P, what *further* causal work is left for M, or the law connecting M and P? This is a form of "the exclusion problem;" see below for further discussion.
7. Brian McLaughlin calls this "type epiphenomenalism" in "Type Epiphenomenalism, Type Dualism, and the Causal Priority of the Physical," *Philosophical Perspectives* 3 (1989): 109–135.
8. Jerry A. Fodor, "Making Mind Matter More," *Philosophical Topics* 17 (1989): 59–80. In his "Thinking Causes" (in *Mental Causation,* ed. Heil and Mele), Davidson seems to buy into Fodor's proposal. To see why this won't work, at least for Davidson, see note 6 above.

9. Ernest LePore and Barry Loewer, "Mind Matters," *Journal of Philosophy* 93 (1987): 630–642.

10. Terence Horgan, "Mental Quausation," *Philosophical Perspectives*, 3 (1989): 47–76.

11. Davidson, "Thinking Causes," in *Mental Causation*, ed. Heil and Mele. For an earlier attempt to make use of supervenience to explain mental causation, see my "Epiphenomenal and Supervenient Causation," *Midwest Studies in Philosophy* 9 (1984): 257–270; reprinted in *Supervenience and Mind*. I explain why I now think this approach to be inadequate in *Supervenience and Mind*, pp. 358–362.

12. See Stephen P. Stich, *From Folk Psychology to Cognitive Science* (Cambridge: MIT Press, 1983).

13. For a clear development of these issues, see Ned Block, "Can Mind Change the World?" in *Meaning and Method*, ed. George Boolos (Cambridge: Cambridge University Press, 1990).

14. For a more detailed statement of this argument, see Stephen P. Stich, "Autonomous Psychology and the Belief-Desire Thesis," *The Monist* 61 (1978): 573–591.

15. There are well-known considerations supporting a view of this kind; see, for example, Hilary Putnam, "The Meaning of 'Meaning'," in *Philosophical Papers*, vol. 2 (Cambridge: Cambridge University Press, 1975); Tyler Burge, "Individualism and the Mental," *Midwest Studies in Philosophy* 4 (1979): 73–121; Stich, "Autonomous Psychology and the Belief-Desire Thesis;" Kim, "Psychophysical Supervenience," *Philosophical Studies* 41 (1982): 51–70.

16. Due to the works by Hilary Putnam, Saul Kripke, Tyler Burge, and others.

17. For instructive and helpful discussion of issues concerning the causal/explanatory efficacy of contentful mental states, see Lynne Rudder Baker, *Explaining Attitudes* (Cambridge: Cambridge University Press, 1995), and Pierre Jacob, *What Minds Can Do* (Cambridge: Cambridge University Press, 1997).

18. *Psychosemantics* (Cambridge: MIT Press, 1987), p. 42.

19. Terence Horgan, "Supervenient Qualia," *Philosophical Review* 96 (1987): 491–520.

20. On content externalism, wide-content states will not supervene on internal physical properties of the subject, but physicalists will not deny that they supervene on the subject's extrinsic/relational physical properties. For the present paper, we will ignore the issues that arise from content externalism. But see the works by Baker and Jacob cited in note 17.

21. On this issue see my "Postscripts on Mental Causation" in *Supervenience and Mind* (Cambridge: Cambridge University Press, 1993).

22. Strictly speaking, this doesn't go far enough: it must further be the case that one instance causes another instance *in virtue of the fact that the first is of an F-instance and the second is a G-instance.*

23. This argument is based on what I have called "the principle of causal/ explanatory exclusion"; see, for example, my "Mechanism, Purpose, and Explanatory Exclusion," reprinted in *Supervenience and Mind*.

24. We could have begun with (vi) as our initial premise of mental causation. The point of starting with (iii) is to show that the argument applies to mental-mental causation as well as to mental-physical causation. On the assumption of mind-body supervenience, the former is as problematic, in my view, as the latter.

25. This of course is not to assume transitivity for counterfactuals in general.

26. One philosopher who holds the unorthodox view that the base properties "cause" the supervenient properties is John Searle, in his *The Rediscovery of the Mind* (Cambridge: MIT Press, 1992).

27. Note, however, that these regularities are likely to be restricted in generality. The reason is that M's alternative supervenience bases cannot be counted on to cause P^* and hence M^*.

28. On the distinction between "causal process" and "pseudo-process," see Wesley Salmon, *Scientific Explanation and the Causal Structure of the World* (Princeton: Princeton University Press, 1984).

29. Several philosophers have raised exactly these questions (though not necessarily directed against our first argument); for example, Lynne Rudder Baker, "Metaphysics and Mental Causation," in *Mental Causation*, ed. Heil and Mele (Oxford: Clarendon Press, 1993); Robert Van Gulick, "Three Bad Arguments for Intentional Property Epiphenomenalism," *Erkenntnis* 36 (1992); Louise M. Antony, "The Inadequacy of Anomalous Monism as a Realist Theory of Mind," in *Language, Mind, and Epistemology*, ed. G. Preyer, F. Siebelt, and A. Ulfig (Dordrecht: Kluwer, 1994).

30. John R. Searle, *The Rediscovery of the Mind* (Cambridge: MIT Press, 1992).

31. *The Rediscovery of the Mind*, p. 107.

32. *The Rediscovery of the Mind*, p. 87.

33. In "Consciousness, the Brain and the Connection Principle: A Reply," *Philosophy and Phenomenological Research* 55 (1995): 217–232. The quoted passages are from p. 219.

34. In the quotation Searle says "the same system," not "the same situation." But it is clear that saying the former isn't enough; he must say the latter for his reply to have the intended effect.

35. "Making Mind Matter More"; the quoted passage occurs on p. 66.

36. On this point, however, see my discussion of "program explanation" in chapter 3.

37. "Can the Mind Change the World?"

38. Well, sort of. As he points out in the paper, Block has been ambivalent about functionalism for many years. Although he has done much to clarify the functionalist doctrines and lend them coherence and plausibility, he is also responsible for some of the most telling objections against functionalism. I believe this isn't really a matter of ambivalence; it seems to me that Block

is drawn to functionalism for cognitive mental states but has difficulty seeing how it can work for sensory/qualitative states ("qualia")—a position not unlike what I espouse in these lectures.

39. "Can the Mind Change the World?" p. 159.

40. Except possibly for the causal antecedents of the color itself.

41. For similar reasons Elizabeth Prior, Robert Pargetter, and Frank Jackson argue for the causal impotence of dispositions, in their "Three Theses About Dispositions," *American Philosophical Quarterly* 19 (1982): 251–257.

42. More exactly: ". . . causes property *K* to be instantiated" or "causes events of kind *K*." For brevity, the simpler expression will often be used.

43. Block credits Jerry Fodor with this suggestion. It would seem that this could happen only if sleep caused cancer, and this means that dormitivity is causally sufficient for cancer only because each of its realizer is. In a slightly different context (at the 1997 Oberlin Philosophy Colloquium) Louise Antony raised a point similar to Fodor's.

44. In "Multiple Realization and the Metaphysics of Reduction" reprinted in *Supervenience and Mind*.

45. Whether the principle is to be stated in terms of identity or inclusion will depend on how "realizer" is understood. On a plausible construal if *P* is a realizer of *F*, then any stronger property *P** (say, *P & Q*, for a nontrivial *Q* consistent with *P*) is also a realizer of *F*, and *P** may have stronger causal powers than *P*, powers that we may not wish to attribute to the instance of *F* in question. This raises many interesting questions which we cannot pursue here. The main point, though, is that an instance of a second-order property cannot have causal powers beyond those of the realizing property involved.

46. For example, see Sydney Shoemaker, "Causality and Properties," reprinted in his *Identity, Cause, and Mind* (Cambridge: Cambridge University Press, 1984). Also see Fodor's *Psychosemantics* where he defends the principle that scientific kinds are individuated by causal powers.

47. In "The Individuation of Events," reprinted in his *Essays on Actions and Events*, Davidson advocates an individuation principle for events according to which events with the same causal relations are one and the same event.

48. I am indebted to Martin Jones and David Sosa for their probing comments on some points in this chapter that have helped me to improve it.

Notes to Chapter 3

1. But not entirely; see, for example, Richard Swinburne, *The Evolution of the Soul* (Oxford: Clarendon, 1986); W. D. Hart, *The Engines of the Soul* (Cambridge: Cambridge University Press, 1988); John Foster, *The Immaterial Self* (London: Routledge, 1991).

2. I try to reconstruct this derivation in "Psychophysical Laws," reprinted in *Supervenience and Mind* (Cambridge: Cambridge University Press, 1993).

3. See the beginning of chapter 2.
4. Tyler Burge, "Mind-Body Causation and Explanatory Practice," in *Mental Causation*, ed. John Heil and Alfred Mele (Oxford: Clarendon, 1993), p. 97. See also a shorter discussion in his "Philosophy of Language and Mind: 1950–1990," *Philosophical Review* 101 (1992): 3–51 (see pp. 36–39).
5. Burge, "Mind-Body Causation and Explanatory Practice," p. 118.
6. Lynne Rudder Baker, "Metaphysics and Mental Causation," in *Mental Causation*, ed. Heil and Mele, pp. 92–93.
7. Although I think Burge goes too far when he says "Epiphenomenalism is often taken as a serious metaphysical option," pp. 102–103, there have been philosophers fitting his description: see, for example, Peter Bieri, "Trying out Epiphenomenalism," *Erkenntnis* 36 (1992): 283–309, and Frank Jackson and Philip Pettit's "program explanation" discussed below.
8. Burge, p. 103.
9. See, for example, A. I. Melden, *Free Action* (London: Routledge and Kegan Paul, 1961); A. R. Louch, *Explanation and Human Action* (Oxford: Blackwell, 1968); William H. Dray, *Laws and Explanations in History* (Oxford: Oxford University Press, 1957).
10. See Donald Davidson, "Actions, Reasons, and Causes," *Journal of Philosophy* 60 (1963), reprinted in his *Essays on Actions and Events* (Oxford: Cleared Press, 1980). More recently noncausalism has gained new advocates; in particular, see George Wilson, *The Intentionality of Human Action* (Stanford: Stanford University Press, 1989), and Carl Ginet, *On Action* (Cambridge: Cambridge University Press, 1990).
11. See the papers cited in chapter 2, note 5.
12. See for details my "Mechanism, Purpose, and Explanatory Exclusion," *Philosophical Perspectives* 3 (1989): 77–108; reprinted in *Supervenience and Mind* (Cambridge: Cambridge University Press, 1993).
13. Burge, p. 116.
14. Burge, p. 116.
15. "Kim on Mental Causation and Causal Exclusion," *Philosophical Perspectives* 11 (1997).
16. Baker, p. 93.
17. Burge, p. 115.
18. Baker, p. 93.
19. David Lewis is an exception, but to eliminate such "back-tracking counter-factuals," Lewis has to deploy some heavy-duty metaphysical armor. See Lewis, "Counterfactual Dependence and Time's Arrow" and "Causation," both reprinted in his *Philosophical Papers* II (New York and Oxford: Oxford University Press, 1986).
20. For further discussion of the counterfactual approach, see my *Philosophy of Mind* (Boulder, CO: Westview, 1996), pp. 139–144.

21. Frank Jackson and Philip Pettit, "Program Explanation: A General Perspective," *Analysis* 50 (1990): 107–117. See also their "Functionalism and Broad Content," *Mind* 97 (1988): 381–400.

22. Jackson and Pettit, "Program Explanation: A General Perspective," p. 114.

23. Ibid.

24. Jackson and Pettit, pp. 115–116.

25. David Lewis, "Causal Explanation," in his *Philosophical Papers* II (Oxford: Oxford University Press, 1986), p. 217.

26. Lewis of course works with his special notion of causal dependence defined in terms of counterfactuals. But we can make use of the broad ideas Lewis introduces, leaving open the specifics, such as an exact definition of causal dependence, to be settled to suit one's preferences in such matters.

27. Burge, p. 102.

28. Baker, p. 77.

29. Robert Van Gulick, "Three Bad Arguments for Intentional Property Epiphenomenalism," *Erkenntnis* 36 (1992), p. 325.

30. William G. Lycan, *Consciousness* (Cambridge: MIT Press, 1987), p. 38 (emphasis in the original).

31. Block, "Can the Mind Change the World?"

32. Block, "Can the Mind Change the World?," p. 168, note 9. He says that this is a "real physical possibility," citing Hans Dehmelt, "Triton, . . . electron, . . . cosmos, . . . : An infinite regression?" *Proceedings of the National Academy of Sciences* 96 (1986): 8618; and "Experiments on the structure of an individual elementary particle," *Science* 247 (1990): 539–545.

33. David Armstrong, *A Theory of Universals*, vol. 2 (Cambridge: Cambridge University Press, 1978), ch. 18.

34. To make this more precise: the a_is, P_is, and R are implicitly existentially quantified in the definiens.

35. My thanks to David Chalmers, Martin Jones, and David Sosa for helpful comments on the materials of this chapter.

Notes to Chapter 4

1. Two examples come to mind: Jerry Fodor's project of "naturalizing" content and Fred Dretske's externalist approach to consciousness. See Fodor's *Psychosemantics* (Cambridge: MIT Press, 1987) and Dretske's *Naturalizing the Mind* (Cambridge: MIT Press, 1995). "Naturalization" doesn't offend, it seems, in the way "reduction" does.

2. See Robert Causey, *Unity of Science* (Dordrecht: Reidel, 1977).

3. An additional reason for wanting bridge laws to be biconditionals is to open the possibility of identifying properties of the theory being reduced with their coextensions in the base theory, for obviously unless F and G are at least coextensive, they cannot be identical.

4. Notably Jerry Fodor, "Special Sciences, or the Disunity of Science as a Working Hypothesis," *Synthese* 28 (1974): 97–115.
5. In particular, in his "Thinking Causes," in *Mental Causation*, ed. John Heil and Alfred Mele (Oxford: Clarendon, 1993).
6. In this way, then, Davidson's antireductive argument generalizes to all the special sciences too. But this presumably is not an intended result. In fact, if we are allowed to begin with the nonexistence of strict laws outside basic physics as a premise, we can cut away all the complex and obscure arguments Davidson marshalls in "Mental Events" and elsewhere for mental anomalism and reach the desired conclusion in a single step. For since strict laws can exist only in basic physics, there of course cannot be strict laws in psychology or between psychology and anything else!
7. These are possible responses only to the availability question arising from considerations of multiple realization. Obviously they are not relevant to Davidsonian anomalism.
8. For example, Terence Horgan, "Kim on Mental Causation and Causal Exclusion," *Philosophical Perspectives* 11 (1997): 165–184.
9. I believe that this is one real source of both the anomalousness of psychology and the existence of reasonably reliable psychological regularities. No humans are exactly alike physically, and there are always substantial anatomical-physiological differences as in members of any species. We have to expect—we in fact know—that these differences will show up in mental differences, and we cannot expect exceptionless, lawful psychological regularities. This is consistent with each individual's psychology being wholly determined by his/her physiology and being entirely nomological taken in itself. Species-wide human psychology yields no exceptionless laws, only statistical regularities for the same reason that there are no universal laws applicable to, say, all automobiles, not even to all tokens of the 1992 Toyota Camry.
10. This approach to reduction and reductive identification is implicit in David Armstrong's argument for central-state materialism in his *A Materialist Theory of the Mind* (London: Routledge and Kegan Paul, 1968). See also Robert Van Gulick, "Nonreductive Materialism and the Nature of Intertheoretic Constraint," in *Emergence or Reduction*, ed. Ansgar Beckermann, Hans Flohr and Jaegwon Kim (Berlin: De Gruyter, 1992), and Joseph Levine, "On Leaving out What It's Like," in *Consciousness*, ed. Martin Davies and Glyn W. Humphreys (Oxford: Blackwell, 1993).
11. The following question would have occurred to astute readers at this point: If M is an extrinsic/relational property and P (presumably) isn't, how can they be one and the same property? A good question! In the terminology of "role" and "occupier," this question can be rephrased as follows: If M is a causal role and P its occupant, how could M and P be the same property? How could roles be identical with their occupants? We will discuss this issue later.

12. I am using "level" in its customary sense, not in my special sense in which "level" is contrasted with "order." Thus, for example, purely derivational reductions like the reduction of Kepler's laws to Newtonian laws do not fall under the model being described here.

13. This apparently assumes that identity of properties is independent of the laws (and causal relations) in which they figure, and there is a tension between this assumption and the view, which will later come into play, that scientific kinds and properties are fundamentally individuated in terms of their causal powers. I believe that the two views can be reconciled but must set this issue aside for another occasion.

14. Saul Kripke, *Naming and Necessity* (Cambridge: Harvard University Press, 1980).

15. Brian McLaughlin makes this point in his "The Rise and Fall of British Emergentism," in *Emergence or Reduction?*.

16. For more details see my "Making Sense of Emergentism," forthcoming.

17. See Putnam, *Representation and Reality* (Cambridge: MIT Press, 1988; John R. Searle, *The Rediscovery of the Mind*.

18. See, for example, David Chalmers, *The Conscious Mind* (Oxford: Oxford University Press, 1996).

19. I believe that others (perhaps, Shoemaker and Block) have made a similar observation.

20. This claim is disputed by qualia externalists; see Fred Dretske, *Naturalizing the Mind* (Cambridge: MIT Press, 1995), and Michael Tye, *Ten Problems of Consciousness* (Cambridge: MIT Press, 1995).

21. You may recall the logical jokes in *Alice in Wonderland* based on such errors.

22. See, for example, Jerry Fodor, *Psychosemantics* (Cambridge: MIT Press, 1987).

23. Again I must set aside the problem of dealing with multiple realization in the proposed scheme. A hint of how I would proceed is contained in my "Postscripts to Mental Causation," in *Supervenience and Mind*.

24. See, for example, David Armstrong, *A Theory of Universals*, vol. 2 (Cambridge: Cambridge University Press, 1978), ch. 14.

25. This therefore is a hitherto unnoticed kind of counterexample to the D-N model of explanation as it is standardly formulated, such as by Carl G. Hempel and Paul Oppenheim in "Studies in the Logic of Explanation," in Hempel, *Aspects of Scientific Explanation* (New York: Free Press, 1965).

26. For more details, see my "Multiple Realization and the Metaphysics of Reduction," reprinted in *Supervenience and Mind*.

27. For some interesting further considerations against the disjunctive approach, see Louise Antony and Joseph Levine, "Reduction with Autonomy," *Philosophical Perspectives* 11 (1977): 83–105.

28. The case for this is made stronger if we also assume that kinds and properties in science must be individuated in terms of causal powers, a principle often assumed in discussions of the issues under discussion. See, for example, Sydney Shoemaker, "Causality and Properties," in *Identity, Cause, and*

Mind (Cambridge: Cambridge University Press, 1984); Jerry Fodor, *Psychosemantics;* and my "Multiple Realization and the Metaphysics of Reduction" in *Supervenience and Mind.* But this additional assumption is not needed.

29. One could argue that the vocabulary in which H is to be specified is a *conceptual* issue not an issue about properties.
30. I seem to remember David Armstrong making this point.
31. See the end of chapter 2.
32. Also between *determination* and *explanation.* As we saw in our discussion of reduction, emergentists would accept that emergent properties are determined by basal conditions but deny that the basal conditions can explain why just these emergent properties emerge from them.
33. For some more details on these issues, see my "Making Sense of Emergence," forthcoming.
34. Samuel Alexander, *Space, Time, and Deity* (London: Macmillan, 1920), vol. 2, p. 8.
35. The reductive physicalist would say that reductionism does retain mentality as a distinctive part of the physical domain, but its distinctiveness is physical distinctiveness, not some nonphysical distinctiveness.
36. I benefited from questions and comments by David Chalmers and David Sosa.

References

Alexander, Samuel. *Space, Time, and Deity*, vol. 2. London: Macmillan, 1920.

Antony, Louise, M. "Anomalous Monism and the Problem of Explanatory Force." *Philosophical Review* 98 (1989): 153–187.

Antony, Louise, M. "The Inadequacy of Anomalous Monism as a Realist Theory of Mind." In *Language, Mind, and Epistemology*, ed. G. Preyer, F. Siebelt, and A. Ulfig. Dordrecht: Kluwer, 1994.

Antony, Louise M., and Joseph Levine. "Reduction with Autonomy." *Philosophical Perspectives* 11 (1997): 83–105.

Armstrong, David. *A Materialist Theory of Mind*. New York: Humanities Press, 1968.

Armstrong, David. *A Theory of Universals*, vol. 2. Cambridge: Cambridge University Press, 1978.

Baker, Lynne Rudder. "Metaphysics and Mental Causation." In *Mental Causation*, ed. Heil and Mele.

Baker, Lynne Rudder. *Explaining Attitudes*. Cambridge: Cambridge University Press, 1995.

Beckermann, Ansgar, Hans Flohr, and Jaegwon Kim, eds. *Emergence or Reduction?* Berlin: De Gruyter, 1992.

Bieri, Peter. "Trying out Epiphenomenalism." *Erkenntnis* 36 (1992): 283–309.

Block, Ned. "Can the Mind Change the World?" In *Meaning and Method*, ed. George Boolos. Cambridge: Cambridge University Press, 1990.

Block, Ned. "Introduction: What Is Functionalism?" In *Readings in Philosophy of Psychology*, vol. 1, ed. Block. Cambridge: Harvard University Press, 1980.

Block, Ned. "Anti-Reductionism Slaps Back." *Philosophical Perspectives* 11 (1997): 107–132.

Broad, C. D. *The Mind and Its Place in Nature*. London: Routledge and Kegan Paul, 1925.

Burge, Tyler. "Mind-Body Causation and Explanatory Practice." In *Mental Causation*, ed. John Heil and Alfred Mele.

Burge, Tyler. "Individualism and the Mental." *Midwest Studies in Philosophy* 4 (1979): 73–121.

Burge, Tyler. "Philosophy of Language and Mind: 1950–1990." *Philosophical Review* 101 (1992): 3–51.

Causey, Robert. *Unity of Science*. Dordrecht: Reidel, 1977.

Chalmers, David. *The Conscious Mind*. Oxford: Oxford University Press, 1996.

Davidson, Donald. "Mental Events." 1970. Reprinted in Davidson, *Essays on Actions and Events*.

Davidson, Donald. *Essays on Actions and Events*. Oxford: Oxford University Press, 1980.

Davidson, Donald. "Actions, Reasons, and Causes." *Journal of Philosophy* 60 (1963). Reprinted in *Essays on Actions and Events*.

Davidson, Donald. "The Individuation of Events." Reprinted in *Essays on Actions and Events*.

Davidson, Donald. "Psychology as Philosophy." Reprinted in *Essays on Actions and Events*.

Davidson, Donald. "Thinking Causes." In *Mental Causation*, ed. John Heil and Alfred Mele.

Descartes, René. *The Philosophical Writings of Descartes*, vol. 2, ed. John Cottingham, Robert Stoothoff, and Dugald Murdoch. Cambridge: Cambridge University Press, 1985.

Dray, William H. *Laws and Explanations in History*. Oxford: Oxford University Press, 1957.

Dretske, Fred. *Naturalizing the Mind*. Cambridge: MIT Press, 1995.

Endicott, Ronald. "Constructive Plasticity." *Philosophical Studies* 74 (1994): 51–75.

Feigl, Herbert. "The 'Mental' and the 'Physical'." *Minnesota Studies in the Philosophy of Science*, vol. 2, ed. Herbert Feigl, Grover Maxwell, and Michael Scriven. Minneapolis: University of Minnesota Press, 1958.

Fodor, Jerry A. "Special Sciences, or the Disunity of Science as a Working Hypothesis." *Synthese* 28 (1974): 97–115. Reprinted in *Representations*.

Fodor, Jerry A. "Making Mind Matter More." *Philosophical Topics* 17 (1989): 59–79. Reprinted in *A Theory of Content and Other Essays*. Cambridge: MIT Press, 1990.

Fodor, Jerry A. *Representations*. Cambridge: MIT Press, 1981.

Ginet, Ginet. *On Action*. Cambridge: Cambridge University Press, 1990.

Goldberg, Bruce. "The Correspondence Hypothesis." *Philosophical Review* 77 (1968): 439–454.

Heil, John. *The Nature of True Minds*. Cambridge: Cambridge University Press, 1992.

Heil, John, and Alfred Mele, eds. *Mental Causation*. Oxford: Clarendon, 1993.

Hempel, Carl G., and Paul Oppenheim. "Studies in the Logic of Explanation." Reprinted in Hempel, *Aspects of Scientific Explanation*. New York: Free Press, 1965.

Honderich, Ted. "The Argument for Anomalous Monism." *Analysis* 42 (1982): 59–64.

Horgan, Terence. "From Supervenience to Superdupervenience." *Mind* 102 (1993): 555–586.

Horgan, Terence. "Supervenience and Cosmic Hermeneutics." *Southern Journal of Philosophy* 22 (1984), suppl: 19–38.

Horgan, Terence. "Mental Quausation." *Philosophical Perspectives* 3 (1989): 47–76.

Horgan, Terence. "Supervenient Qualia." *Philosophical Review* 96 (1987): 491–520.

Horgan, Terence. "Kim on Mental Causation and Causal Exclusion." *Philosophical Perspectives* 11 (1997): 165–184.

Horgan, Terence, and Mark Timmons. "Troubles on Moral Twin Earth: Moral Queerness Revisited." *Synthese* 92 (1992): 221–260.

Jackson, Frank, and Philip Pettit. "Functionalism and Broad Content." *Mind* 97 (1988): 381–400.

Jackson, Frank, and Philip Pettit. "Program Explanation: A General Perspective." *Analysis* 50 (1990): 107–117.

Jacob, Pierre. *What Minds Can Do.* Cambridge: Cambridge University Press, 1997.

Kim, Jaegwon. "Does the Problem of Mental Causation Generalize?" *Proceedings of the Aristotelian Society* 97 (1997): 281–297.

Kim, Jaegwon. "Psychophysical Laws." Reprinted in *Supervenience and Mind.*

Kim, Jaegwon. "What is the Problem of Mental Causation?" *Norms and Structures in Science,* ed. M. L. Dalla Chiara et al. (Dordrecht: Kluwer, 1997).

Kim, Jaegwon. "Concepts of Supervenience." Reprinted in *Supervenience and Mind.*

Kim, Jaegwon. "Mental Causation: What? Me Worry?" *Philosophical Issues* 6 (1995): 123–151.

Kim, Jaegwon. "Epiphenomenal and Supervenient Causation." *Midwest Studies in Philosophy* 9 (1984): 257–270. Reprinted in *Supervenience and Mind.*

Kim, Jaegwon. "Mechanism, Purpose, and Explanatory Exclusion." *Philosophical Perspectives* 3 (1989): 77–108. Reprinted in *Supervenience and Mind.*

Kim, Jaegwon. "Multiple Realization and the Metaphysics of Reduction." Reprinted in *Supervenience and Mind.*

Kim, Jaegwon. "Psychophysical Supervenience." *Philosophical Studies* 41 (1982): 51–70. Reprinted in *Supervenience and Mind.*

Kim, Jaegwon. "Self-Understanding and Rationalizing Explanations." *Philosophia Naturalis* 82 (1984): 309–20.

Kim, Jaegwon. "The Myth of Nonreductive Physicalism." *Proceedings and Addresses of the American Philosophical Association* 63 (1989): 31–47. Reprinted in *Supervenience and Mind.*

Kim, Jaegwon. "The Nonreductivist's Troubles with Mental Causation." In *Supervenience and Mind.*

Kim, Jaegwon. "'Downward Causation' in Emergentism and Nonreductive Physicalism." In *Emergence or Reduction?,* ed. A. Beckermann, H. Flohr, and J. Kim.

Kim, Jaegwon. "'Strong' and 'Global' Supervenience Revisited." Reprinted in *Supervenience and Mind.*

Kim, Jaegwon. "Supervenience as a Philosophical Concept." Reprinted in *Supervenience and Mind.*

Kim, Jaegwon. *Supervenience and Mind.* Cambridge: Cambridge University Press, 1993.

Kim, Jaegwon. *Philosophy of Mind.* Boulder, CO: Westview, 1996.

Kim, Jaegwon. "The Mind-Body Problem after 50 Years." Delivered at the Royal Institute of Philosophy, October, 1996.

Kim, Jaegwon. "The Mind-Body Problem: Taking Stock after 40 Years," *Philosophical Perspectives,* 11 (1997): 185–207.

Kim, Jaegwon. "Making Sense of Emergence." Presented at the 1997 Oberlin Colloquium in Philosophy (forthcoming in *Philosophical Studies*).

Kripke, Saul. *Naming and Necessity.* Cambridge: Harvard University Press, 1980.

LePore, Ernest, and Barry Loewer. "Mind Matters." *Journal of Philosophy* 93 (1987): 630–642.

Levine, Joseph. "On Leaving out What It's Like." In *Consciousness,* ed. Martin Davies and Glyn W. Humphreys. Oxford: Blackwell, 1993.

Lewis, David. "Counterfactual Dependence and Time's Arrow." Reprinted in *Philosophical Papers* II. Oxford: Oxford University Press, 1986.

Lewis, David. "Causal Explanation." In *Philosophical Papers* II. Oxford: Oxford University Press, 1986.

Lewis, David. "Causation." Reprinted in *Philosophical Papers* II.

Louch, A. R. *Explanation and Human Action.* Oxford: Blackwell, 1968.

Lycan, William G. *Consciousness.* Cambridge: MIT Press, 1987.

Malcolm, Norman. *Memory and Mind.* Ithaca: Cornell University Press, 1977.

Marr, David. *Vision.* New York: Freeman Press, 1982.

McLaughlin, Brian. "Type Epiphenomenalism, Type Dualism, and the Causal Priority of the Physical." *Philosophical Perspectives* 3 (1989): 109–135.

McLaughlin, Brian. "Varieties of Supervenience." In *Supervenience: New Essays,* ed. E. Savellos and Umit D. Yalcin. Cambridge: Cambridge University Press, 1995.

McLauglin, Brian. "The Rise and Fall of British Emergentism." In *Emergence or Reduction?,* ed. Beckerman, Flohr, and Kim.

Melden, A. I. *Free Action.* London: Routledge and Kegan Paul, 1961.

Morgan, C. Lloyd. *Emergent Evolution.* London: Williams and Norgate, 1923.

Nagel, Ernest. *The Structure of Science.* New York: Harcourt, Brace, 1961.

Oppenheim, Paul, and Hilary Putnam. "Unity of Science as a Working Hypothesis." *Minnesota Studies in the Philosophy of Science,* vol. 2, ed. H. Feigl, G. Maxwell, and M. Scriven. Minneapolis: University of Minnesota Press, 1958.

Place, U. T. "Is Consciousness a Brain Process?" *British Journal of Psychology* 47, Part I (1956): 44–50.

Post, John. *The Faces of Existence.* Ithaca: Cornell University Press, 1987.

Prior, Elizabeth, Robert Pargetter, and Frank Jackson. "Three Theses About Dispositions." *American Philosophical Quarterly* 19 (1982): 251–257.

Putnam, Hilary. "The Meaning of 'Meaning'." In *Philosophical Papers,* vol. 2. Cambridge: Cambridge University Press, 1975.

Putnam, Hilary. "On Properties." In *Philosophical Papers,* vol. 1. Cambridge: Cambridge University Press, 1975.

Putnam, Hilary. "Psychological Predicates." First published in 1968 and later Reprinted under the title "The Nature of Mental States." In Putnam, *Collected Papers* II. Cambridge: Cambridge University Press, 1975.

Putnam, Hilary. "Minds and Machines." In *Dimensions of Mind*, ed. Sydney Hook. New York: New York University Press, 1960.

Putnam, Hilary. *Representation and Reality*. Cambridge: MIT Press, 1988.

Ryle, Gilbert. *The Concept of Mind*. London: Hutchinson and Company, Ltd., 1949.

Salmon, Wesley C. *Scientific Explanation and the Causal Structure of the World*. Princeton: Princeton University Press, 1984.

Savellos, Elias, and Umit Yalcin, eds. *Supervenience: New Esays*. Cambridge: Cambridge University Press, 1995.

Searle, John R. *The Rediscovery of the Mind*. Cambridge: MIT Press, 1992.

Searle, John R. "Consciousness, the Brain and the Connection Principle: A Reply." *Philosophy and Phenomenological Research* 55 (1995): 217–232.

Shoemaker, Sydney. "Some Varieties of Functionalism." Reprinted in *Identity, Cause, and Mind*. Cambridge: Cambridge University Press, 1984.

Shoemaker, Sydney. "Causality and Properties." Reprinted in *Identity, Cause, and Mind*. Cambridge: Cambridge University Press, 1984.

Smart, J. J. C. "Sensations and Brain Processes." *Philosophical Review* 68 (1959): 141–156.

Sosa, Ernest. "Mind-Body Interaction and Supervenient Causation." *Midwest Studies in Philosophy* 9 (1984): 271–81.

Stich, Stephen P. *From Folk Psychology to Cognitive Science*. Cambridge: MIT Press, 1983.

Stich, Stephen P. "Autonomous Psychology and the Belief-Desire Thesis." *The Monist* 61 (1978): 573–591.

Stoutland, Frederick. "Oblique Causation and Reasons for Action." *Synthese* 43 (1980): 351–67.

Tye, Michael. *Ten Problems of Consciousness*. Cambridge: MIT Press, 1995.

Van Gulick, Robert. "Three Bad Arguments for Intentional Property Epiphenomenalism." *Erkenntnis* 36 (1992).

Van Gulick, Robert. "Nonreductive Materialism and the Nature of Intertheoretic Constraint." In *Emergence or Reduction*, ed. Beckermann, Flohr, and Kim.

Varela, Francisco, Evan Thompson, and Eleanor Rosch. *The Embodied Mind*. Cambridge: MIT Press, 1993.

von Wright, G. H. *Explanation and Understanding*. Ithaca: Cornell University Press, 1971.

Wilson, George. *The Intentionality of Human Action*. Stanford: Stanford University Press, 1989.

Index